APPLIED ECONOMICS ON NORTH-EAST INDIA

APPLIED ECONOMICS ON NORTH-EAST INDIA

Dr. Kanchan Datta
Dr. Chandan Kumar Mukhopadhyay

ABHIJEET PUBLICATIONS
DELHI 110094

ABHIJEET PUBLICATIONS
2/46 Tukhmeerpur Extension
Delhi-110 094
Phone: 011-22960492, 65698474
E-mail: abhijeetpublication@gmail.com

APPLIED ECONOMICS ON NORTH-EAST INDIA

First Published 2011

ISBN 978-93-81136-17-1

PRINTED IN INDIA

Published by J.K. Singh for Abhijeet Publications, Delhi-110 094, Lasertypeset by Gaurav Graphics, New Delhi and Printed at Himanshu Printers, Delhi.

Preface

North-east India consists of eight states: Assam, Arunachal Pradesh, Manipur, Meghalaya, Mizoram, Nagaland, Tripura and finally Sikkim, these are popularly known as seven sisters and one brother. There has been a plethora of research studies regarding the economy, socio-cultural structure, political boundary, ethnicity, terrorism of North-East India. There has been a huge promise regarding the development of these states, both from central and state governments' corner. But inspite of this promise with respect to development perspective it is still far below to South India, West India and North India. It is not that north east states are resource less. Inspite of having plenty of potential resources why these states are not flourishing is a matter of research. This book basically seeks to investigate the relationship between two macro economic variables, contribution of forestry and fishing, overall development indicators and present status compared to national average, tourism potentialities, forecasting on domestic tourists arrival etc. We shall be very happy if this book benefits any researchers, government officials or political leaders. We shall gladly accept any comments or suggestions for the improvement of this book.

Finally, we express our sincere gratitude to Professor A. Basumajumdar, Hon'ble Vice Chancellor, North Bengal University, since he is our main source of inspiration of accelerating the pace of research activities. We are also grateful to Abhijeet Publications for taking the initiative of publication of this book.

Dr. Kanchan Datta

&

Dr. Chandan Kumar Mukhopadhyay

Contents

1

Relationship between Agriculture and Economic Growth in Arunachal Pradesh—A Reflection of Tribal Commitment

1.1 Introduction

India has the largest concentration of tribal people anywhere in the world except perhaps in Africa. The tribal are children of nature and their lifestyle is conditioned by the Eco-system. India, with a variety of ecosystems, presents a varied tribal population throughout its length and breadth. The areas inhabited by the tribal constitute a significant part of the under developed areas of the country. The tribal live mostly in isolated villages or hamlets. A smaller portion of their population has now settled in permanent villages as well as in towns and cities. On the whole, as per rough estimates, the prominent tribal areas constitute about 15 percent of the total geographical area of the country. Tribal people over the years have become the most disadvantaged, exploited and the neglected lot in our society. The tribal basically stand averse to the modern life styles and hardly willing to change until and unless they encounter a very strong social mobilization.

There are 533 tribes (with many overlapping types in more than one State) as per notified Schedule under Article 342 of the Constitution of India in different States and Union Territories of the country with the largest number of 62 being in the State of Orissa.

Arunachal Pradesh is a thinly populated hilly tract lying on the north-east extremity of India comprising roughly 83,573 square kilometers. The Pradesh is known to be rich in flora, fauna, power and mineral potential. Previously this region was known as the North East Frontier Agency (NEFA) and constituted a part of the state of Assam. Arunachal Pradesh became an independent state on 20th February 1987. It is bounded by independent countries on the three sides and by Assam and Nagaland in the south. The long international border comprises of Bhutan on its west (160 km), the Tibet region of China on its northern and north east border (1080 km) and Myanmar (formerly Burma (440km) on the eastern border.

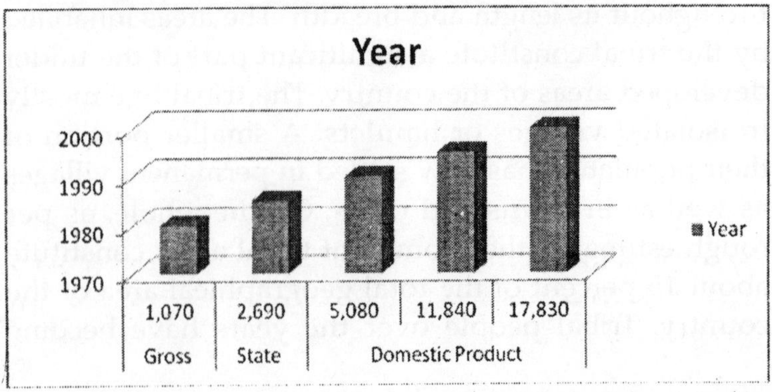

Arunachal Pradesh's gross state domestic product for 2004 was estimated at $706 million in current prices. Agriculture primarily drives the economy. Jhum, the local word for a shifting cultivation widely practiced among the tribal groups, is now less practiced. Arunachal Pradesh has close to 61,000 square kilometers of forests, and forest products are the next most significant sector of the economy. Among the crops grown here are rice, maize, millet, wheat, pulses, sugarcane, ginger, and oilseeds. Arunachal is also ideal for horticulture and fruit orchards. Its major industries are rice mills, fruit preservation units, and handloom handicrafts. Saw-mills and plywood trades are prohibited under law.

1.2 Some of the major Tribes of North Eastern India

Arunachal Pradesh: Nyishi, Adi, Tagin, Apatani, Wangcho, Dafla, Khampti, Singpho etc

Assam: Boro, Kachari, Mikir (Karbi), Lalung, Rabha, Dimasa, Hmar, Hajong etc

Meghalaya: Garo, Khasi, Jayantia, etc.

Tripura: Chakma, Garo, Khasi, Kuki, Lusai, Liang, Santhal etc

Mizoram: Lusai, Kuki, Garo, Khasi, Jayantia, Mikir etc.

According to 2001 Census, in Arunachal Pradesh the tribal population constitutes 64.22% of the total population in which the highest percentage is in Kurung Kurney district with (97.89%) while in Lohit district schedule tribes account for only a third of the population (32.42). Figure-1.1 shows the diagrammatic representation of the tribal peoples in

North-Eastern states in India. Which shows that Mizoram, Meghalaya and Nagaland contain more than 80% of schedule tribe people.

Figure 1.1

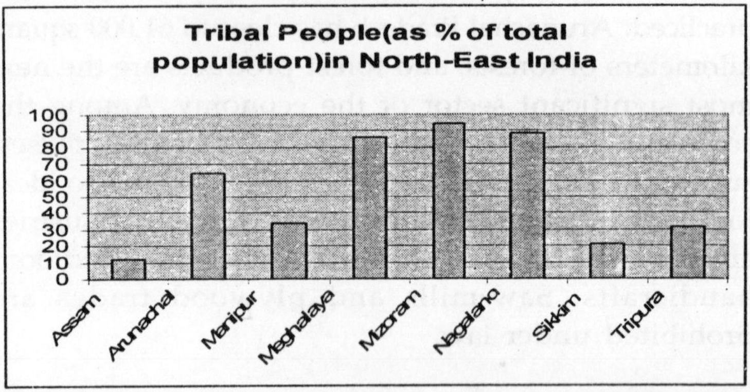

In 1990, an attempt was taken by UNDP in its Human Development Reports to construct an index to analysis the comparative status of socio-economic development of different nations, which is termed as 'Human Development Index' (HDI). The HDI attempts to rank all countries on a scale of 0 to 1. It consists of three indices, income index, health index and education index. With respect to HDI Arunachal Pradesh is the least developed states among eight north-eastern states in India.

Other than HDI, there are other indices to measure level of development from various angles these are GDI (Gender Development Index), GEM (Gender Empowerment Index), HPI (Human Poverty Index) etc, according to GDI nation's development can not be possible without the development of female. The main components of these index is

(1) with respect to per-capita income how much females are getting compared to male

(2) with respect to education how girl students are progressing compared to boys

(3) the male-female ratio with respect to enrollment in school and

(4) average life expectancy of female compared to male etc.

Therefore according to this index though high HDI implies high level of development, but it does not reflect the status of women of a nation. It is only through GDI which reflects the status of women of a nation and whose development is the true reflection of the development of a nation. Some socio-economic indicators are given in the table below.

Table 1.1

States	*Population Growth (1991-2001)*	*Area (Sq.Km)*	*Literacy rate (2001)*		*HDI*		
			Male	*Female*	*1981*	*1991*	*2001*
India	22.7		75.8	54.2	0.263	0.381	0.56
Arunachal	27	83743	63.8	43.5	0.228	0.328	0.49
		(B)	(L)	(L)	(L)	(L)	(L)

Table 1.1 shows with respect to decadal population growth Arunachal is higher than national average, where as with respect to literacy rate, it is lagging behind the national average both with respect to male and female. The Human Development Index shows its rank is lowest among the eight north-east states in India.Figure-1.2 shows the sectoral share of Gross State Domestic Product (GSDP), which clearly shows the share of agriculture has declined slightly between 1999 to 2005, where as the share of service sector has increased while intermediate sector remains unchanged.

Figure 1.2

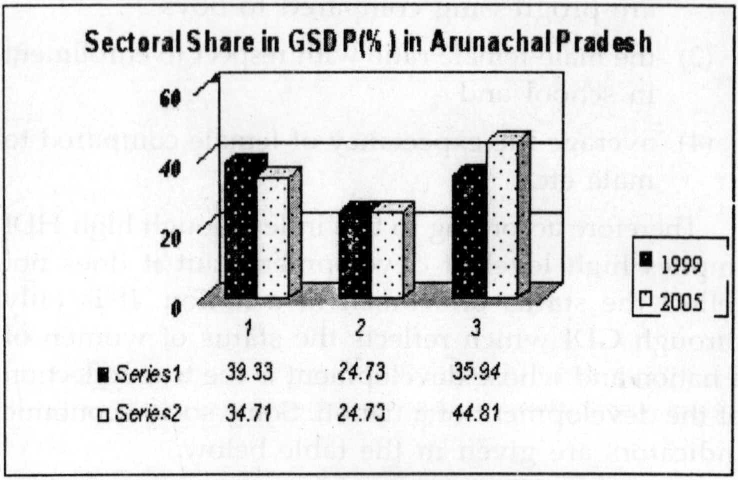

1.3 Objective and Importance of the Study

Since a huge percentage of tribal people in Arunachal Pradesh depended on agriculture and its related activities and the remaining are in unregistered manufacturing hence the objective of this study is to investigate the contribution of agriculture and its related activities that is finishing, forestry and logging, village industries (Unregistered manufacturing) to the growth of state's income (NSDP). This may be a true reflection of the tribal people's commitment to the growth of state's income.

1.4 Data and Methodology

In this study the data are time series yearly data taken from RBI bulletin and the time periods are from 1999 to 2007. As far as methodology is concerned Vector Auto Regression (VAR) models are used.

1.5 Models

The study is based on the following equations. Where g means growth rate.

$gNSDP_t = \alpha_1 + \alpha_2\ gNSDPt\text{-}1 + \alpha_3\ gNSDP_{t-2} + \alpha_4\ gFISHING_{t-1} + \alpha_5\ gFISHING_{t-2} + \varepsilon_1$ (1.1)

$gFISHING_t = \beta_1 + \beta_2\ gNSDP_{t-1} + \beta_3\ gNSDP_{t-2} + \beta_4\ gFISHING_{t-1} + \beta_5\ gFISHING_{t-2} + \varepsilon_2$ (1.2)

$gNSDP_t = \gamma_1 + \gamma_2\ gNSDP_{t-1} + \gamma_3\ gNSDP_{t-2} + \gamma_4\ gMANUFAC_{t-1} + \gamma_5\ gMANUFAC_{t-2} + \varepsilon_3$ (1.3)

$gMANUFAC_t = \delta_1 + \delta_2\ gNSDP_{t-1} + \delta_3\ gNSDP_{t-2} + \delta_4\ gMANUFAC_{t-1} + \delta_5\ gMANUFAC_{t-2} + \varepsilon_4$ (1.4)

$gNSDP_t = \theta_1 + \theta_2\ gNSDP_{t-1} + \theta_3\ gNSDP_{t-2} + \theta_4\ gFORESTRY_{t-1} + \theta_5\ gFORESTRY_{t-2} + \varepsilon_5$ (1.5)

$gFORESTRY_t = \pi_1 + \pi_2\ gNSDP_{t-1} + \pi_3\ gNSDP_{t-2} + \pi_4\ gFORESTRY_{t-1} + \pi_5\ gFORESTRY_{t-2} + \varepsilon_6$ (1.6)

$gNSDP_t = \mu_1 + \mu_2\ gNSDP_{t-1} + \mu_3\ gNSDP_{t-2} + \mu_4\ gAGRI_{t-1} + \mu_5\ gAGRI_{t-2} + \varepsilon_7$ (1.7)

$gAGRI_t = \upsilon_1 + \upsilon_2\ gNSDP_{t-1} + \upsilon_3\ gNSDP_{t-2} + \upsilon_4\ gAGRI_{t-1} + \upsilon_5\ gAGRI_{t-2} + \varepsilon_8$ (1.8)

where ε_i i=1…8 are white noise error terms

1.6 Diagrammatic Presentation of the Primary and Unregistered Manufacturing Industries

Figure 1.3 shows the diagrammatic representation of the growth of agriculture and its related activities and the growth of unregistered manufacturing.

Figure 1.3

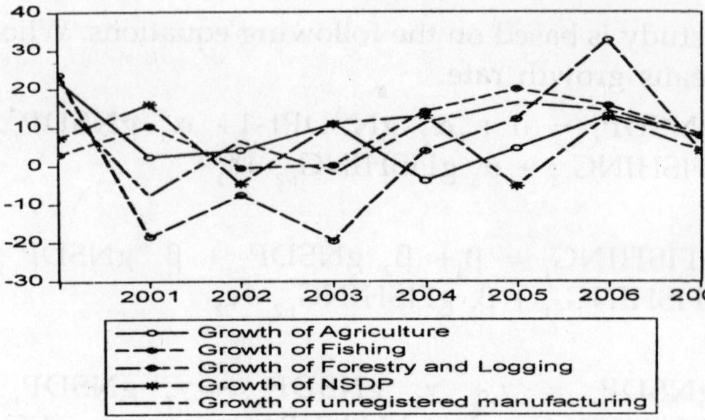

Figure 1.3 shows the diagrammatic representation of the Agricultural growth and its related activities and the growth of unregistered manufacturing, since in Arunachal Pradesh there is not a single registered manufacturing sector, so unregistered manufacturing may be treated as village and small industries. The common thing among the entire growth rate is that volatility, that is growth, is fluctuating in nature. The growth of agriculture has a declining trend, where as growth of fishing, forestry and logging have an upward tendency. But after 2006 all the rates have sharply declined.

1.7 Findings

The estimations of the VAR model is given in the table below. For equations (1.1) and (1.2) that is

$$gNSDP_t = \alpha_1+\alpha_2\, gNSDP_{t-1}+ \alpha_3\, gNSDP_{t-2}+ \alpha_4\, gFISHING_{t-1} + \alpha_5\, gFISHING_{t-2} +\varepsilon_1 \quad (1.1)$$

$$gFISHING_t=\beta_1+\beta_2 gNSDP_{t-1}+\beta_3 gNSDP_{t-2}+\beta_4 gFISHING_{t-1} + \beta_5\, gFISHING_{t-2} +\varepsilon_2 \quad (1.2)$$

Table 1.2: Results of Regression of Equations (1.1) and (1.2)

Constant / Parameters	*Estimated value*	*Standard error*	*t-value*	*Level of Significance*
α_1	22.12701	2.06508	10.7148	***
α_2	-1.254897	0.13250	-9.47069	***
α_3	-0.867919	0.12173	-7.12975	***
α_4	-0.059800	0.10901	-0.54860	
α_5	-0.310992	-3.85247	-2.33296	**
β_1	19.58160	0.69644	1.49250	
β_2	-0.895403	-5.53169	-1.06364	
β_3	-0.810697	0.77340	-1.04823	
β_4	1.017424	0.69254	1.46912	
β_5	-1.140936	0.84691	-1.34717	

*** implies 1% level, ** implies 5% level of significance

Now for equations (1.3) and (1.4) that is

$$gNSDP_t = \gamma_1+\gamma_2\, \gamma NSDP_{t-1}+ \gamma_3\, gNSDP_{t-2}+\gamma_4\, gMANUFAC_{t-1} +\gamma_5\, gMANUFAC_{t-2} +\varepsilon_3 \quad (1.3)$$

$$gMANUFAC_t = \delta_1+\delta_2\, gNSDP_{t-1}+ \delta_3\, gNSDP_{t-2} + \delta_4\, gMANUFAC_{t-1} + \delta_5\, gMANUFAC_{t-2} +\varepsilon_4 \quad (1.4)$$

Table 1.3: Results of Regression of Equations (1.3) and (1.4)

Constant / Parameters	*Estimated value*	*Standard error*	*t-value*	*Level of Significance*
γ_1	20.71048	3.27120	6.33115	***
γ_2	-1.193590	0.19780	-6.03437	***
γ_3	-0.832517	0.19743	-4.21681	***
γ_4	-0.244023	0.15594	-1.56483	
γ_5	-0.101848	0.15561	-0.65449	

δ_1	2.089404	13.8013	0.15139
δ_2	0.396526	0.83452	0.47516
δ_3	0.138423	0.83295	0.16618
δ_4	0.378914	0.65792	0.57593
δ_5	0.102966	0.65653	0.15683

*** implies 1% level, ** implies 5% level of significance

Now for equations (1.5) and (1.6) that is

$$gNSDP_t = \theta_1+\theta_2\ gNSDP_{t-1}+\theta_3\ gNSDP_{t-2}+\theta_4\ gFORESTRY_{t-1} + \theta_5\ gFORESTRY_{t-2}+\varepsilon_5 \quad (1.5)$$

$$gFORESTRY_t = \pi_1+ \pi_2\ gNSDP_{t-1}+ \pi_3\ gNSDP_{t-2}+\pi_4\ gFORESTRY_{t-1}+ \pi_5\ gFORESTRY_{t-2} +\varepsilon_6 \quad (1.6)$$

Table 1.4: Results of Regression of Equations (1.5) and (1.6)

Constant / Parameters	*Estimated value*	*Standard error*	*t-value*	*Level of Significance*
θ_1	18.30712	1.04608	17.5007	***
θ_2	-1.147456	0.07678	-14.9443	***
θ_3	-0.853194	0.07889	-10.8154	***
θ_4	-0.126980	0.02856	-4.44547	***
θ_5	-0.028704	0.03428	-0.83728	
π_1	6.184676	30.8081	0.20075	
π_2	-0.281858	2.26132	-0.12464	
π_3	-0.016277	2.32331	-0.00701	
π_4	0.358167	0.84124	0.42576	
π_5	0.080458	1.00964	0.07969	

*** implies 1% level, ** implies 5% level of significance

Finally for equations (1.7) and (1.8) that is

$$gNSDP_t = \mu_1+ \mu_2\ gNSDP_{t-1}+ \mu_3\ gNSDP_{t-2}+ \mu_4\ gAGRI_{t-1} + \mu_5\ gAGRI_{t-2} +\varepsilon_7 \quad (1.7)$$

$$gAGRI_t = \upsilon_1 + \upsilon_2\, gNSDP_{t-1} + \upsilon_3\, gNSDP_{t-2} + \upsilon_4\, gAGRI_{t-1} + \upsilon_5\, gAGRI_{t-2} + \varepsilon_8 \qquad (1.8)$$

Table 1.5: Results of Regression of Equations (1.7) and (1.8)

Constant / Parameters	*Estimated value*	*Standard error*	*t-value*	*Level of Significance*
μ_1	59.36616	10.7938	5.50005	***
μ_2	-3.852477	0.69644	-5.53169	***
μ_3	-3.806143	0.77413	-4.91664	***
μ_4	-2.635494	0.68232	-3.86253	***
μ_5	1.451465	0.37053	3.91726	***
υ_1	-55.92007	26.2779	-2.12803	**
υ_2	3.614995	1.69551	2.13210	**
υ_3	4.700092	1.88467	2.49386	**
υ_4	3.986752	1.66115	2.40000	**
υ_5	-1.943655	0.90207	-2.15465	**

*** implies 1% level, ** implies 5% level of significance

From the above results it can be said,

(1) Regarding equation (1.1) and (1.2) α_2 and α_3 are highly significant; it implies current period growth of income inversely depends on previous two period's income. It is the reflection of volatility of income.

(2) α_5 is also significant, which implies two previous periods growth of fishing is also significant for maintaining the volatility of income growth.

(3) β_i's are insignificant, it implies growth of income is not significant for the growth of fishing, it is totally traditional year after year.

(4) γ_4, γ_5 and δi's are insignificant, which implies neither income growth affecting manufacturing nor the unregistered manufacturing growth affecting growth of income. Therefore manufacturing is at the subsistence level.

(5) θi's are significant . It shows that a large section of tribal people are dependent on forest resources. Growth of forestry and logging is significantly affecting the growth of income.

(6) Finally the growth of income positively affecting the growth of agriculture.

1.7 Conclusion

In the eighties and latter half of nineties agriculture's contribution was more prominent than the growth of any other states. Nowadays almost 32% Arunachal's economic growth comes from Agriculture. Forestry and logging, and Fisheries take an important part in the economy of Arunachal Pradesh. The primary sector as a whole recently is responsible for 40% of the economic growth of the state. But the average contribution of manufacturing is being 4.04% of NSDP. If this situation continues it will be very difficult for the government of Arunachal to raise the level of development indices.

REFERENCES

Arunachal Pradesh Human Development Report, 2003.

Reserve Bank of India Bulletin Published Data (Down Load)

India Development Report, 2005.

Nayak, Purusottam. 'Human Development Reports on North-East India: A Bird's Eye View': (Down Load)

National Human Development Report, 2001.

Reserve Bank of India Bulletin (Sectoral Composition of NSDP)

Todaro M.P. and Smith S.C. *Economic Development,* Eight editions, 2003

Tripura Human Development Report, 2003.

2

Tourism in Arunachal Pradesh—Some Prospects and Problems

2.1 Introduction

Tourism has become one of the most flourishing industries in the world. Today, it is the second largest and fastest growing industry, next only to the petroleum industry. Worldwide, tourism is emerging as one of the biggest employers compared to any other economic sector. It offers opportunities for economic, cultural and political exchanges, generates employment, foreign exchange and raises living standards. It facilitates social integration and international understanding.

2.2 Tourism Economics

Tourism can play an important, pioneering and effective role in achieving the growth targets set out for the nation. The primary objective of tourism development in India is to accelerate economic growth significantly, so as to meet a series of socio-economic imperative that are unique to India.

The National Action Plan for Tourism (1992), defines the objectives of tourism development in India and the primary strategy for its development:

a. It is a unifying and a nation-building force, through fostering greater national and international understanding, particularly amongst the youth of the country.
b. It serves to preserve and enrich India's cultural heritage.
c. It brings socio-economic benefits.

The strategy for achieving these objectives has been outlined as:

a. Improvement of tourist infrastructure.
b. Developing areas on a selective basis for integrated growth, along with the marketing of destinations on the basis of a 'Special Tourism Area' concept.
c. Restructuring and strengthening of institutions for development of human resources.
d. Evolving a suitable policy for increasing foreign tourist arrivals and foreign exchange earnings.

2.3 Tourism development in Northeast India

It is unfortunate that due to socio-political and geographical reasons, the entire Northeast has remained neglected and backward from the development point of view. In spite of very high literacy rate in the region (around 80%), progress and benefits have not reached the Northeast even today.

The concept of Tourism development is very recent in this region and is in its infancy. A few states like Sikkim and Assam have taken a few strides in developing tourism, with emphasis on eco-tourism, wildlife tourism, cultural tourism and adventure tourism. The other states have also commenced their efforts during the last decade.

However, the tourism development of the Northeast region needs to be targeted via a regional approach rather than an individual state approach. The basic needs for tourism development of the region are efficient infrastructure, good connectivity between the states and peace in the region. The entry permit formality required for a few states for both domestic and international tourists is a major deterrent to the region's tourism attractiveness.

2.4 Positive & Negative Factors of North-East Region

General Negative Factors of NE Region:

(1) Insurgency, Isolated/Neglected & Backward region,

(2) Adverse climatic conditions, particularly in monsoon,

(3) Earthquake prone region, Inappropriate Time Zone,

(4) Poor communication infrastructure/ connectivity to mainland and also within the NE states,

(5) Poor development infrastructure: power, roads, industry, transportation, (6) Lack of higher/ Professional education & research facilities,

(7) Jhoom cultivation causing degradation of natural resources,

(8) Lack of emergency medical facilities. Loss of ethnic culture especially in the hilly region,

(9) Lack of exposure to the outside world, finally

(10) Lack of professionalism in attitude and management.

General Positive Factors of NE Region

(1) Wonderful Natural Beauty of Mountains and Rivers,

(2) Unique and endemic flora and fauna, large percentage of land under forest cover,

(3) Low population density,

(4) Clean and unpolluted Environment,

(5) Closeness to five international boundaries—Nepal, Bhutan, China, Myanmar and Bangladesh,

(6) Diversity of very charming ethnic cultures, Diversity of folk art forms particularly music and dances,

(7) Hospitality and warmth of people,

(8) Great potential for Eco-tourism, Adventure Tourism, and Religious Tourism.

2.5 Objectives of the Study

Assess the existing tourism scenario in Arunachal Pradesh with respect to natural resources, heritage and other socio-cultural assets, quantitative and demographic factors such as population, employment, occupation, income levels, services and infrastructure.

2.6 Global Tourism Trends

Tourism is today the world's largest industry, with the Travel and Tourism (T & T) Industry and T & T Economy respectively contributing 4.2% and 10.7% of global GDP. Tourism is also the highest generator of jobs, with the T & T Economy accounting for 8.2% of total employment or 1 in every 12.2 jobs. By 2011, over 50 million additional jobs will be created by the T & T Economy. No wonder then that Tourism has been described as 'one of the most remarkable economic and social phenomena of the last century'.

International tourism has grown steadily since 1950, as also tourism expenditure. The revenue from international tourism means a lot to the host country as it is contributed by foreign visitors in foreign exchange. This becomes very useful for the host country for its economic and infrastructure development. The World Tourism Organization (WTO) estimates that international tourist arrivals will exceed 160 crores by the year 2020.

Tourism has become so important and competitive that about 150 countries have set up National Tourist Organizations to attract foreign tourists to their countries and also to encourage their own people to travel within their own country. The following table will provide a global picture (2000) of the region-wise tourists arrivals and earnings of some countries in the world tourism.

Figure 2.1

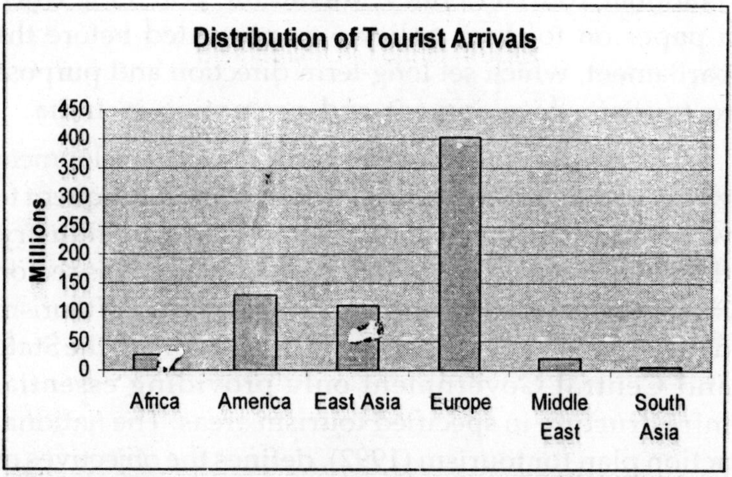

(*Source:* WTO)

Figure 2.2

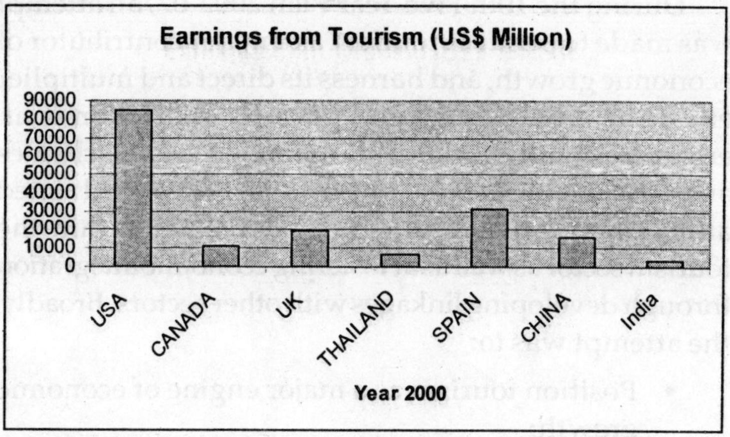

(*Source:* WTO)

2.7 Tourism Policy in India

Economic planning in India has followed the system of five-year plans. Tourism found no mention in the first five-year plan. The first attempt to formulate a

'National Tourism Policy' was in the year 1982 when a paper on tourism policy was presented before the parliament, which set long-term direction and purpose to tourism development and promotion in India.

The vast potential and the need for rapid development was recognized only in the seventh plan, subsequent to which tourism was accorded the status of an Industry, thereby encouraging private investments in this sector. In subsequent plans the primary responsibility of tourism development was with the private sector with the State and Central Government only providing essential infrastructure in specified tourism areas. The national action plan for tourism (1992), defines the objectives of tourism development in India and the primary strategy for development.

During the 10th Five Year Plan 2002-07, an attempt was made to position tourism as a major contributor of economic growth, and harness its direct and multiplier effects for employment and poverty eradication in an environmentally sustainable manner. Various schemes and activities taken up during the 10th Plan period aimed at enhancing the employment potential within the tourism sector as well as at fostering economic integration through developing linkages with other sectors. Broadly, the attempt was to:

- Position tourism as a major engine of economic growth;
- Harness the direct and multiplier effects of tourism for employment generation, economic development and providing impetus to rural tourism;
- Focus on Domestic Tourism as a major driver of tourism growth;

- Position India as a global brand to take advantage of the burgeoning global travel and trade and the vast untapped potential of India as a destination;
- Acknowledge the critical role of private sector with government working as a pro-active facilitator and catalyst;
- Create and develop integrated tourism circuits based on India's unique civilization, heritage, and culture in partnership with States, private sector and other agencies.

2.8 A Brief History of Arunachal Pradesh

There is not much information available on the history of Arunachal Pradesh. The earliest recorded history dates back to 16th century AD when Ah m rulers of Assam extended their kingdom to this region. The Ahom rulers had a tradition of not interfering in the affairs of the tribes of this region. The British continued this policy, and in 1873, they banned entry of outsiders to this region. The Government of India continued this policy until 1962, when China attacked this region. After 1962, steps were taken to counter future border disputes with China, and roads, electricity, modern democratic institutions, and cash economy were introduced here.

Before 1962, the state was known as Northeast Frontier Agency and was constitutionally a part of Assam. Because of its strategic importance, it was administered by the Ministry of External Affairs until 1965 and subsequently by the Ministry of Home Affairs through the governor of Assam. In 1972, Arunachal Pradesh was constituted as a union territory, and, in 1987, it became the 24th state of the Indian Union.

2.9 Connectivity

a) Road

Arunachal Pradesh State Transport Corporation operates regular bus-services to various places in Arunachal Pradesh and its neighbouring states. Direct bus-services are there from North Lakhimpur to Itanagar via Naharlagun. Itanagar is also connected by daily buses from Guwahati (429 km).

b) Rail

The nearest railway station is Harmuty (near Banderdewa check gate) in Assam only 23 km from Naharlagun and 33 km from Itanagar. However nearest convenient railhead is North Lakhimpur in Assam, 50 km from Naharlagun and 60 km from Itanagar.

c) Air

Nearest airport is in Lilabari (North Lakhimpur) in Assam, 57 km from Naharlagun and 67 km from the capital, Itanagar. Indian Airlines operates direct flight from Calcutta to Tezpur (216 km from Itanagar). There are helicopter services available from Guwahati to Naharlagun.

Permit:

Indian tourists visiting Arunachal require mandaterily an "Inner Line Permit" from the Arunachal Government office at Delhi or Itanagar. Foreign Tourists requires restricted "Area Permit valid" for a maximum stay of 10 days. Places of tourism importance in Arunachal Pradesh are as follows:

2.10 Facts and Figures:

Arunachal Pradesh is the land of tribal groups like Nishi, Mishmi,Mompa, Khamti, etc. The land has not yet tasted the effects of complete urbanization. Though it is a land blessed with varied resources, economy of Arunachal Pradesh has still not attained self-sufficiency. Economy in Arunachal Pradesh depends on the following:

2.11 Agriculture:

In Arunachal Pradesh, 1.10 lakh hectares is under Jhum Cultivation and 0.90 hectares is under permanent cultivation. There are Government Farms in Arunachal Pradesh promoting proper agricultural practices and various institutions like Gramesevak Training Center or Farmers Training Center to guide the farmers. Wheat, millet, rice, pulses, potatoes and sugarcane are the main crops of the state.

2.12 Horticulture :

The climate and topography of Arunachal Pradesh is conducive to horticultural products like ginger, spices, bamboo, cardamom and mushroom, aromatic and medicinal plants.

2.13 Industry:

There are 5 District Industrial Centers and 8 Sub-District Industrial Centers in Arunachal Pradesh. There are a number of saw mills, plywood factories, petro-chemical industries, hydro-electric projects, cement factories in Arunachal Pradesh. The minerals found here are coal, dolomite, lead, zinc, graphite and marble.

2.14 Forestry:

About 61,000 sq km of Arunachal Pradesh is covered with thick forests. The types of forests found here are:

- Tropical Forests
- Sub-Tropical Evergreen Forests
- Temperate Forests
- Pine Forests
- Bamboo Forests

Theses forests support the industrialization in Arunachal Pradesh.

- Livestock in Arunachal Pradesh: The livestocks are the sources of milk, meat, manure, egg and transportation in rural areas; thus contributing to the family as well as state's economy. In recent years, pisciculture has also become an important source of employment and income in Arunachal Pradesh.
- Tourism in Arunachal Pradesh: The adventurous sports and scenic beauty of the land draws thousands of tourists every year, ushering tourism industry a prolific growth and stabilizing the economy of Arunachal Pradesh.

2.15 Tourism Scenario in Arunachal Pradesh:

Figure 2.3

Arunachal Pradesh is on the northeastern tip of India, largest of the seven sisters of North East India bordering Bhutan on the west, China on the north, Myanmar on the east and the states of Assam on the south. Part of the Eastern Himalayan ranges, this state covers 83,743 sq. km., with climate varying from sub-tropical in the south to alpine in the north. Evergreen forest covers more than 60 % of the state area. Besides the streams, rivers, mountains and peaks, its' endless variations of scenic beauty are the first to greet sunrise in the country.

. It finds mention in the ancient literature such as the Kalika Purana, the Mahabharata and the Ramayana. It was here that Parasuram washed away his sins, Vyasa meditated, Bhismaka founded his kingdom, Lord Krishna married his consort Rukmini, and King Balinarayan drew men for his armies from among the hardy people. The 6th Dalai Lama was born and the 13th found refuge on the soil of Arunachal Pradesh.

2.16 Identified Tourist Spots in Arunachal Pradesh:

Figure 2.4

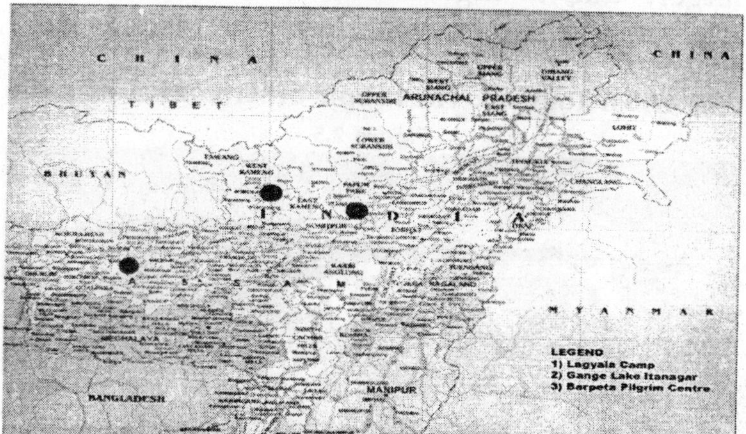

Arunachal Pradesh is a thinly populated hilly tract lying in the north-east extremity of India comprising roughly 83,573 kilometer square of area. It is known for rich in flora, fauna, power and mineral potential. It has Bhutan on its west, the Tibet region of China on its northern border and Myanmar on the eastern border. The Brahmaputra, India's major river enters Arunachal Pradesh from Tibet. Arunachal Pradesh, North-East India's remotest state, also known as Land of the "Dawn-lit-Mountains" is the first Indian soil to greet the morning sun.

There are 16 districts, 57 Community Development Blocks 3649 villages. Most of the villages become inaccessible in the monsoon and winter 868429 rural populations and only 222,668 urban populations, 63.65 percent scheduled tribes, literacy rate 54.74 percent (2001, Census Report), male 64.07 percent female 44.24 percent. (Sex ratio is 901 females for 1000 males (2001, Census Report). Arunachal Pradesh registered a high population growth of 36.8 percent (in 1981-91) higher than the all-India growth rate of 23.6 percent. This is largely due to high natural growth and illegal infiltration from Myanmar, Nepal and Bangladesh.

2.17 Tribal Tourism: The People of Arunachal Pradesh:

Figure 2.5

Arunachal has 26 major tribes and many subtribes living in 3649 scattered villages. Although a number of tribal groups constitute the total population, the density of population is very less. They have a rich cultural heritage. The people are simple, friendly and hospitable. Their colourful festivals are manifestations of their faith and belief.

There are three kinds of religions practised here. Monpas and Sherdak Pens in Kameng and Tawang district who came in contact with Tibetan in the north, adopted Lamaism of the Buddhist faith, while the Khamptis in Lohit district practice Mahayana Buddhism. The second group, Noctes and Wanchos in Tirap district, whose long association with the Assamese in the south, converted them to Hinduism. The third group comprises of Adi, Abas, Apatanis, Nyishi, etc.—a large majority of the total population, who maintain their ancient belief and indigenous concepts of nature and worship the Donyi-Polo.

Art and Craft/ Dress and Design:

Artistic craftsmanship in Arunachal has been passed on from one generation to the other. The Buddhist tribes make beautiful masks. They also periodically stage pantomimes and masked dances. They make exquisite carpets, painted wooden vessels and silver articles. People from the central part of the state are expert in cane and bamboo. They weave articles that are in common use in their daily lives. The shawls and jackets, shoulder bags and coats all stand for the perfection that the people have attained in this art. The people of the southeastern part of the territory are famous for their wooden carvings. They weave beautiful bags and loincloths too. Goat's hair, ivory, beads of agate and other stones as well as of brass and glass are the specialties of the people of this part of the region.

The womenfolk throughout the territory have an excellent sense of colour. The basic colours that dominate the weaver are black, yellow, dark blue, green and scarlet—all put together in the most fascinating combinations. The weaving designs are essentially geometric varying from a formal arrangement to lines and bands.

Most of the domestic requirements are made of cane and Bamboo. Hats, baskets, cane vessels, cane belts—woven and plain, bamboo mugs with carvings, a wide variety of ornaments and jewelry items are all crafted by workmen.

A specialty of the Monpas, the Buddhist community, is carpet weaving, with exotic designs of dragons, geometric and floral patterns. Besides, the Monpa wood carver scoops out beautiful cups, dishes and fruit bowls and magnificent ceremonial masks for dances and pantomimes. The Khamtis carve out beautiful religious images, figures of dancers, toys and other objects.

Crafting ornaments is another art widely practiced by the Arunachalis. Besides multicolored beads, feathers of birds and wings of the green beetles are also used as embellishments. The Akas make bamboo bangles and ear- rings, which are occasionally decorated with various designs. The Monpas also make papers for writing religious prayers etc., from pulp of trees called susko or the paper trees.

Table 2.1: Passion and Rhythm: Fairs and Festivals

Occasion	*Time*	*Places*
Lossar	February/March	Dirang, Tawang, Bomdila
Khan	February	Bomdila
Nyethidow	March	Bomdila, Bhalukpung
Nyokum	February 26	Itanagar, Ziro
Mopin	April 5, 6	Itanagar, Daporijo, Along, Pasighat
Solung	September 1, 2	Itanagar, Along, Pasighat
Dree	July 5	Itanagar, Ziro
Reh	-	-
Si- Donyi	January 6	Daporijo
Boori- Boot	February 6	Daporijo
Aaran	March 7	Pasighat
Tamladu	February 15	Tezu
Sanken	April 15	Tezu
Makar Sankranti	January 14	Parasuram Kund

Losar is the New Years' Celebration of the Monpas. During the five days of festivities, prayers are offered, religious flags are hoisted atop their homes; Buddhist scriptures are read in every home and butter lamps are lit in houses and the campuses.

Reh is essentially associated with the Idu Mishmis, the six-day celebrations' special attraction is the Priest dance.

During Tamladu, the Digaru Mishmis offers prayers to the God of the Earth and the God of the Water. The supreme God Jebmalu is also worshipped.

Khan is significant because of a ceremony where the priest ties a piece of wool around everybody's neck.

During Sangken, people sprinkle water on each other as a sign of merriment.

Smearing of rice powder on each other's face marks the beginning of the five-day celebrations of Mopin.

From highly stylised religious dance-dramas of Buddhists to the martial steps and colourful performances of the Noctes and Wanchos, dances here are the source of real joy. Teams of young girls in perfect rhythmic unison perform the Ponung dance of the Adis. Similar group dances in colourful costumes are performed in the Upper and Lower Subansiri.

2.18 Urban Tourism

In spite of all the charms of nature and wilderness, the main attraction for the majority of tourists is major cities. Urban Tourism is at great advantage due to this universal fact. Interestingly, capital of Arunachal Pradesh has one very charming city, wonderfully located and ideally developed.

2.19 Itanagar: A birds' Eye-View of Itanagar

Figure 2.6

(1) It is the capital of the state. The historical fort called "Ita Fort", dating back to the 14-15 centuries, is a famous tourist spot here.

(2) The legendary Ganga Lake (Gyakar Sinyi) is a beautiful picnic spot, 6 km away from Itanagar, a green forest lake surrounded by primeval vegetation, orchids masses on tall trees, tree ferns provides a small taste of the magnificent forests of the state

(3) In addition, the beautiful yellow roofed Buddhist shrine reflects the extensive Tibetan influence and provides good views of Itanagar and the surrounding countryside. Also,

(4) The Jawaharlal Nehru State Museum provides a kaleidoscope of Arunachal Pradesh with its woodcarvings, local musical instruments, textiles, handicrafts and archeological finds, the workshop in the Handicrafts Centre specializes in traditional cane manufacture. It has a library section also.

2.20 Religious Tourism

Tawang

The Tawang Monastery or Gompa is a 400 year old Buddhist monastery founded by a monk, Mera Lama, a contemporary of the fifth Dalai Lama. The entire monastery is in the nature of a walled city with narrow streets and stone houses wherein over 500 monks dwell. The Tawang Monastery includes an expansive library that is the storehouse of old scriptures, painted tapestries, rare hand written and block-printed manuscripts of religious books and gold lettered Buddhist scriptures. One can gain glimpses of the Tibetan influence here—reflected in the elaborately painted wooden windows and other motifs.

The Tawang Gompa is home to the 18 foot high gilded Buddha statue at the entry gate, which is aesthetically decorated with paintings. The ceiling is painted with Buddhism folklore. Research scholars, Buddhist monks and devotees of different faiths from all over the world visit the Tawang Monastery to chant, pray and meditate in this quiet and sublime retreat.

Figure 2.7

TWANG MONASTERY

It was constructed in the 17th century, houses a big library of holy books, some of which are written in gold letters. Situated atop a ridge and surrounded by thick clouds and mist, it seems to be hanging in ethereal space. One of the most important visits here is the Buddhist Monastery, known as "Galden Namgyel Lhatse". It is one of the largest Lamaseries of Mahayana factions in Asia. There are also beautiful lakes around Tawang. Pankang Teng Tso Lake is a paradise for tourist only 17 Km away from the Twang town. Other incredible lake includes Sangetser Lake and Banggachang Lake.

Bhismaknagar

It is located in Dibang Valley district and is a sacred heritage of the Idu Mishmis. Bhismaknagar was a strong hold of the Chutiyas (12th-16th centuries) but the excavations have been throwing new light on its much earlier antiquities. It stands for the best in the tribal and Aryans way of life.

Parasuram Kund

It is located 13 miles north-east of Tezu,District Headquaters of Lohit district—a growing town, famous for its scenic beauty. Thousand of pilgrims visit this place from all parts of India every year during Parasuram mela held in the month of January.

Akashiganga

In West Siang District, it is a popular sacred place. There is a temple near the road. Traveling 100 meters down through a spiral path, 'the miraculous Kund' is located, where devotees take bath. The place also provides a magnificent bird's eye view of the Brahmaputra River glimmering far below.

2.21 Eco Tourism

Bomdila

Bomdila is a spectacular town and the capital of West Kameng district. Bomdila, situated at a height of 2,530 meters, offers breathtakingly panoramic views of Himalayan landscapes and the snow clad mountain peaks. Bomdila, is home to luscious apple orchards, wild orchids, verdant forests and cascading waterfalls. This area has had strong Tibetan and Buddhist links over many centuries and is home to many Buddhist monasteries called 'Gumphas'. One other place of interest here is the Ethnographic Museum.

Table 2.2: Floral Diversity of Arunachal Pradesh

Plant Species	*No. of Species*
Rhododendrons	52
Oaks	16
Bamboo	35
Canes	20
Orchids	550
Medicinal Plants	500
Pteridophytes	452
Bryophytes	60

Source: Arunachal Pradesh State Bio diversity strategy and Action Plan, State Forest Research Institute,2002 Statistical Report-1999-2000, Department of Environment and Forest, Arunachal Pradesh

Malinithan

Figure 2.8

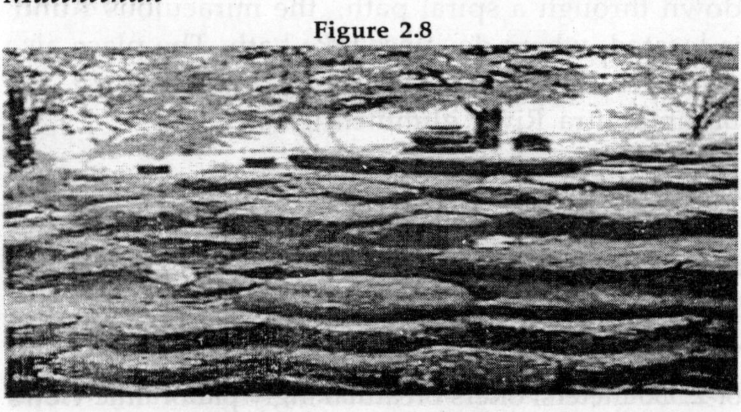

It is a temple site in ruins. It is situated at the foot of the Siang hills under the Likabali Sub-Division of West Siang District of Arunachal Pradesh. It is only 1 Km east of Likabali, the nearest administrative centre. Relics of stone images of Malinithan came to be noted from the early twenties of the present century. In course of series of excavation from 1968 and ending 1971, ruins of temples and valuable scriptures were unearthed at this site. The fame of Malinithan as a holy place of worship draws a large number of visitors and piligrims.

Namdapha

It is located in the Changlang district, and is famous for the wild life sanctuary, which has been declared as a national park. It is a few kilometers away from Miao.

Gange Lake

Figure 2.9

Ganga Lake, a natural lake locally known as "Gyaker Sinyi" (meaning confined water) is only 6 km away from Itanagar, the state capital. It is situated on the foothills of the Himalayas amidst dense forest. The approach road is quite rugged within forest area. It is a beautiful picnic spot for day trip, boating and other recreation. This green forest lake is surrounded by primeval vegetation, orchids, tall trees, ferns, and bamboo groves.

2.22 Adventure Tourism

Arunachal Pradesh is the ideal place for many adventure sports activities like water rafting, boating, kayaking and angling.

Figure 2.10

Wildlife

Given to the topographical and climatic suitability, the woods of Arunachal Pradesh offer a natural habitat for the mammals. Mishmi, Takin, Hoolock Gibbon, Musk Deer, Bharal, Hisbid Hare, Flying Squirrel and more than 500 species of birds are some rare and endangered species of animals and birds which are conserved in two National Parks and four Wildlife Sanctuaries of Arunachal Pradesh Namdhapa National Park, Pakhui Sanctuary, Itanagar Sanctuary, Daying Ering Sanctuary, Mehao Sancuary, Kane Sanctaury, Eagle's Nest Sanctuary, Kamlang Sanctuary, Dibang Sanctuary, Sessa Orchid Sanctuary and Mouling National Park shelters many herbivores and have aided in preserving the many imperiled species of flora and fauna. To name some are Capped Langur, Red panda, Takin, Musk deer, Tiger, Leopard, Snow-leopard, Clouded leopard, Barking Deer, Serow, Honger, Small cats, Black Bear and rare birds.

Five major rivers—Kameng, Subansiri, Siang, Lohit and Tirap—branching out from the ever-flowing Brahmaputra and countless other rivulets meander all over the mystic land of Arunachal Pradesh.

Daporijo is a large fascinating town situated at the confluence of the Sippi and Subansiri rivers - on the right bank of River Subansiri. Places of interest are the local villages in and around the town and a quaint cave a few kilometers away. Daporijo is ideal for trekking and angling in River Subansiri. Daporijo is home to important tribes the Hill Miris, Tagins and Adi-Gallongs. The Adis are very accomplished weavers of cane goods and much of their dexterous skills can be seen in the famous cane suspension bridges of Arunachal Pradesh.

Figure 3 shows the sectoral composition of Income of Arunachal Pradesh.

Figure 2.11

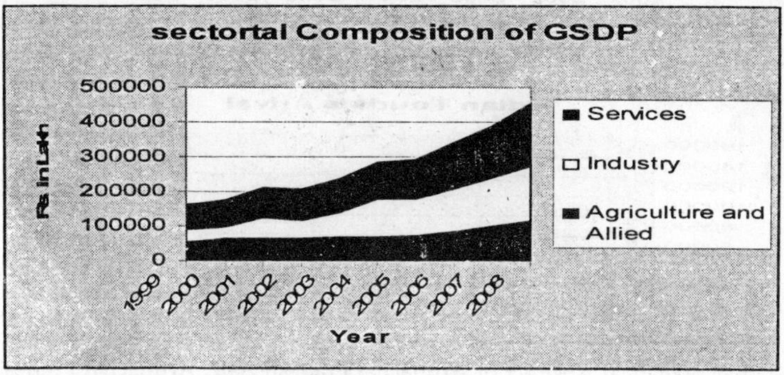

Source: Central Statistical Organization (CSO).

Figure 2.11 clearly shows that the share of service sector is highest compared to primary and secondary sectors.

2.23 Past and Existing Tourism Trends:

Arunachal Pradesh Tourism has maintained records of the tourist arrivals at their tourist lodges. The data provided by the Statistical Abstract of Arunachal Pradesh 2007 gives overall general idea of tourists inflow to the state. It shows a random break up of foreign and domestic tourists. However, destination wise and category wise details of tourist arrivals are not available.

2.24 Arrivals of Tourists in Arunachal Pradesh:

Figure 2.12

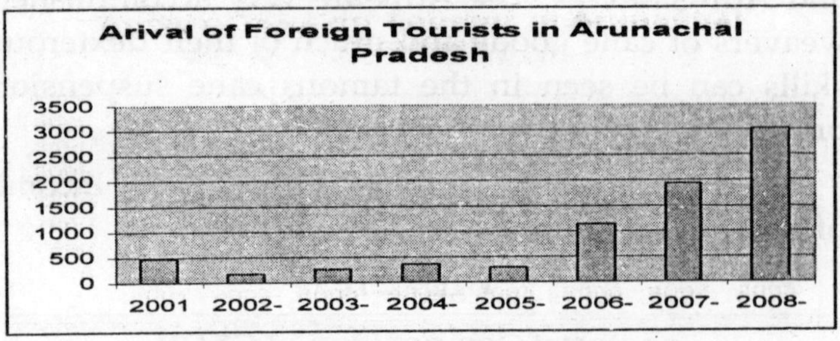

Figure 2.13

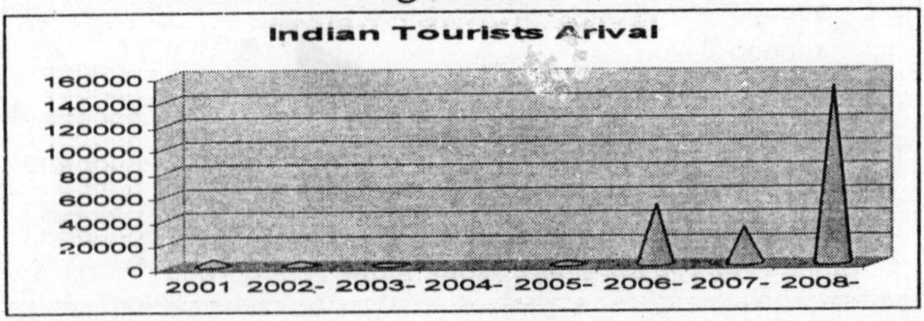

Source: Statistical Abstract of Arunachal Pradesh 2007, Arunachal Pradesh at glance 2009

From figure 2.12 to 2.13 it is clear that the number of foreign as well as Indian tourists have increased in Arunachal Pradesh. These tables clearly indicate an excellent potentiality for the development of this state through tourism. But there are certain threats hindering the development path.

At present the tourist accommodation is scattered all over and not necessarily linked to these destinations. However, this limitation can be used as an opportunity to combine accommodation facilities for various tourist destinations and tourist circuits. A large tourist infrastructure is lying idle today and emphasis must be given to up-grade these facilities and make them functional. The development of innovative tourism destinations combined with appropriate marketing and publicity strategy should attract steady tourist inflow to Arunachal Pradesh. This inflow, in turn, would attract private investments in the hospitality and tourism business.

2.25 Health Infrastructure

Due to remote areas poorly connected by road progress of establishment of health infrastructure has been inadequate. To serve small population groups located at high altitudes without road communication, special sub-centers have been set up with a dai trained to conduct deliveries. Integrating curative services with public health, MCH, FW, with a primary health care approach, Government has been upgrading the existing dispensaries to PHCs, General Hospitals to CHCs and establishing new sub-centers. Rural health infrastructure in Arunachal Pradesh is inadequate particularly in view of very low density of population. At present a PHC is expected to serve an area of

2981 Sq. kms. And sub-centre to serve an area of 186 Sq. km, excluding the sub-centers with volunteer dais. The total number of Government health institute are 255 serving average an area of 327 Sq. km. Establishment of special sub-centers with trained dais is a progressive step to provide basic safe delivery services to remote dwelling population.

Table 2.3: Health Facilities in Arunachal Pradesh

Development of health facilities of Arunachal Pradesh (1961-2001)

Year	Number of Hospitals/ Dispensaries/ Medical Units/ PHCs, etc.	No. of Doctors	No. of Hospital Beds	Population Served per Doctor	No. of Hospitals/ PHCs, etc., per 10,000 Population	No. of Hospital Beds per 10,000 Population
1960-61	77	73	-	4,610	2.287	-
1970-71	122	152	1,190	3,075	2.609	25.45
1980-81	171	256	1,475	2,468	2.706	23.34
1990-91	278	272	2,260	3,155	3.238	26.33
2000-2001	567	464	2,218	2,351	5.196	20.33

Note: Dash means data not available.

Source: Statistical Abstracts of Arunachal Pradesh of different years.

2.26 Conclusion

However looking at the bright tourism potential, enthusiasm of the central government, possible initiative from the state government and the expected rise in tourist arrivals and receipts, it looks quite possible to make tourism in the state sustainable in two decades. It will require futuristic vision, conscious and planned efforts at all levels and a disciplined action plan and implementation strategy. In the meanwhile, sympathetic approach of the central government will be required to stabilize the socio-political situation in the northeast followed by overall infrastructure development in the region.

REFERENCES

Article 371-H-Special provision with respect to the State of Arunachal Pradesh.

Bardhan, Pranab (1995): *The New Institutional Economics and Development Theory Reprinted in Leading Issues in Economic Development*, Gerold M.Meier, and OUP.

Bhattarcharjee, J. B. (2000): *The Eastern Himalayan Trade of Assam in the Colonial Period, In Studies in the History and Culture of Arunachal Pradesh*, Edited by S. Dutta, pp. 269-285, rev-ed. Itanagar, Himalayan Publishers.

Bose, M.L.(1977): *History of Arunachal Pradesh*, New Delhi: Concept Publication.

Census of India (2001): *The State of Arunachal Pradesh*, Government of India.

Chowdhury, J.N. (1973): *Arunachal Panorama*, Shillong: Jaya Choudhury Publication.

Dutta, P. and Ahmand, S.I. (1995): *The People of Arunachal Pradesh: People of India*, Vol. XIV, General Editor K.S.Singhm Calcutta, Seagul Books.

Goswami, M.C. and Das, P.B. (1990): *The People of Arunachal Pradesh: A Physical Survey*, Directorate of Research, Government of Arunachal Pradesh, Itanagar.

Government of Arunachal Pradesh (2004): *Statistical Hand Book of Arunachal Pradesh.*

Government of India (2002): Ministry of Finance: *Economic Survey 2001-2002.*

Helms, M.W. (1993): *Crafts and the Kingly Ideal: Art, Trade and Power*, Austin, University of Texas Press.

Herskovits, M.J. (1952): *Economic Anthropology: A Study in Comparative Economics*, New York.

Jha, S.D. (1986): *Arunachal Pradesh,* New Delhi: Omson Publication.

Kani,T. (1993):*The Advancing Apatanis of Arunachal Pradesh,* Itanagar.

Luthra, P.N. (1993): *Constitutional and Administrative Growth of the Arunachal Pradesh,* Directorate of Research, Government of Arunachal Pradesh.

Ministry of Environment and Forest, *Annual Report 1999-2000.*

NSSO: *Sample Survey 55th Round,* July 1999 to June 2000.

Odi, Dai (1989): *"Property Rights of Women in Arunachal Pradesh,"* Arunachal News Letter, March, 27:3.

Osik, N.N. (1999): *Modern History of Arunachal Pradesh (1825-1997),* Itanagar: Himalayan Publishers.

Ramakrishana, P.S. (1992):*Shifting Agriculture and Sustainable Development,* Paris, UNESCO.

Reserve Bank of India (1983): *Reserve Bank of India: Function and Working,* Bombay.

Reserve Bank of India (2002): *Report on Trend and Progress of Banking in India 2001-2002,* Bombay.

Simon, I. M. (1976): *"The Status of Women in Some North East Indian Tribal Community",* Arunachal News, 4(5):34-39.

Statistical Abstract of India, Government of India.

Usha Sharma (2005). *Discovery of North-East India.* Mittal Publications. p. 65.

World Bank (1987): *Renewal Resources Management in Agriculture,* An Operations Evolution Study.

The Arunachal Times, 19 August 2002.

The Arunachal Times, 25 August 2002.

The Arunachal Times, 18 August 2004.

3

Some Development Indicators in North-East India

Introduction

The northeastern region of India comprising the eight states of Assam, Arunachal Pradesh, Meghalaya, Nagaland, Manipur, Mizoram, Tripura and Sikkim spreads over an extensive area of 262 thousand square km, constituting 8% of total geographical area of the country. This region is known for its bounty of natural resources and admixer of cultures to diverse communities and ethnic groups. This region is enriched with minerals like petroleum, natural gas, coal, uranium etc and also rich in agricultural, horticultural and forest products. Handloom, handicraft, sericulture and hydro power potential also enriched the region. This region is bounded by china and Bhutan in the north and north-west, Myanmar and Bangladesh on its east, south and south west.

The State Assam is rich in arts and crafts skills, is famed for its exemplary silk quality, cane and bamboo items, metal crafts, pottery and woodcrafts and their master artisans. The state Government advances and improves marketability of the products for ensuring livelihood of the stakeholders in the handicrafts and handloom industry through its nodal agencies. Its tourism potential has historical significance. A rich repository of scenic beauty, arts and crafts, dances and theatre, handlooms and handicrafts, rare and rich flora and fauna and places of worship, the State holds the potential of continuing to attract increasing numbers of global tourists. The potential for IT and ITeS industry to grow in Assam lies in the pool of skilled human resources, high literacy and the Government's conscious measures through an IT policy and resolve to build infrastructure. Arguably, tea remains the largest commercial crop for which NER is known worldwide. Assam's tea industry has consistently been a major foreign exchange earner. Assam produces around 53% of India's total production (which is 28% globally) employing more than 10% of the State's work force.

Nagaland has the potential for agro based commercial production for horticulture, floriculture, aromatic and medicinal plant production besides sericulture, animal husbandry and apiculture production to be gainfully tapped tourism, animal husbandry and meat processing are some other promising industries that have the natural potential to develop.

Meghalaya has a hydro-electricity potential of nearly 1,200 MW which is yet to be effectively harnessed. With increased focus on hydro generation in NER, the investment is set to increase. A higher outlay on transportation shows that the government is keen to remove the infrastructural bottlenecks. Agro-horticulture based food processing industry has the potential to develop the State's economy.

A higher outlay on transportation of Tripura shows that the government is keen to remove the infrastructural bottlenecks. Tourism is a major attraction with the State having important temples, several lakes, wild life sanctuaries and 60% natural forest cover. The agro-climatic conditions are favourable for a flourishing food processing industry with the State being a top producer of pineapples. Tripura is second rubber capital in the country with a production at 18,455 TPA. The vast potential for setting up of rubber-based industries is sought to be developed through industrial parks and appropriate fiscal incentives. Bamboo & bamboo handicrafts & products, it and biofuel (jatropa based) are other industries that are being actively developed.

Traditionally there was no difference between the concept 'Economic Growth' and 'Economic Development', by the term 'Economic Growth' of a country meant a sustained or continuous rise in its GNP (at rates 5 to 7% or more).After that it is modified with a sustained rise in per capita GNP, such that the ability of the nation in expanding output should be a greater rate than the rate of growth of its population. Next modification is, it is not per-capita GNP, rather it should be real per capita GNP which is equal to monetary growth of GNP per capita—the rate of inflation, which can be treated as the over all economic well-being of a population.

In the next time period another group of economists opined that the concept of development should be viewed from the angle of production and employment, such that, economic development = growth + structural change, the share of intermediary and tertiary sectors rise at the cost of agriculture with respect to both production and employment perspective. Later on 'social justice' is added in the concept of development. Henceforth economic development is equal to growth + structural change + social justice. Quoting Dudley Seers, "the questions to ask about a country's development are therefore, what has been happening to poverty? What has been happening to unemployment? what has been happening to inequality? if all three of these have declined from high levels, then beyond doubt this has been a period of development for the country concerned . If one or two of these central problems have been growing worse, especially if all the three have, it would be strange to call the result development even if per capita income doubled."

According to Professor A.K. Sen, "capability to function" is what really matters, for identifying a poor or non poor person. As he put it," economic growth can not be sensibly treated as an end in itself. Development has to be more concerned with enhancing the lives we lead and the freedoms we enjoy."

Thus to explain human well-being we have to think beyond the availability of commodities and consider their use , what Sen termed a 'Functioning' that is what a person does with commodities of given characteristics that they come to possess or control. According to A.K Sen Freedom of choice or control of one's own life with self esteem is itself a main aspect of human well-being.

In 1990, an attempt was taken by UNDP in its Human Development Reports to constract an index to analysis the comparative status of socio-economic development of different nations, which is termed as 'Human Development Index' (HDI). The HDI attempts to rank all countries on a scale of 0 to 1. It consists of three indices, income index, health index and education index.

Other than HDI, there are other indices to measure level of development from various angles these are GDI (Gender Development Index), GEM (Gender Empowerment Index), HPI (Human Poverty Index) etc, according to GDI nation's development can not be possible without the development of female. The main components of these index is

(5) with respect to per-capita income how much females are getting compared to male

(6) with respect to education how girl students are progressing compared to boys

(7) the male-female ratio with respect to enrollment in school and

(8) average life expectancy of female compared to male etc.

Therefore according to this index though high HDI implies high level of development, but it does not reflect the status of women of a nation. It is only through GDI which reflects the status of women of a nation and whose development is the true reflection of the development of a nation.

The next instrument to measure development is ITC index or Information Technology and Communication Index. That is development of a nation is highly related with the progress of information technology and communication of the nation. Three items that are counted in this index are,

(i) number of telephone per head (land line)
(ii) number of cell phone per head
(iii) number of persons using internet facilities

UNIDO (United Nations Industrial Development Organization) developed another concept of development through CIP Index that is Competitive Industrial Performance Index. The main factors of this index are

(i) nature of per-capita industrial progress
(ii) per-capita export of industrial product
(iii) nature of technology used in industry that is whether the industrial technology is backdated or latest? It is termed as 'Industrial Intensity' etc.

In spite of having these definitions in 2004, UNCTAD (United Nations Conference on trade and development) has developed another concept which is known as, TDI (Trade and Development Index), composition of TDI can be shown with the help of the chart below.

Figure 3.1

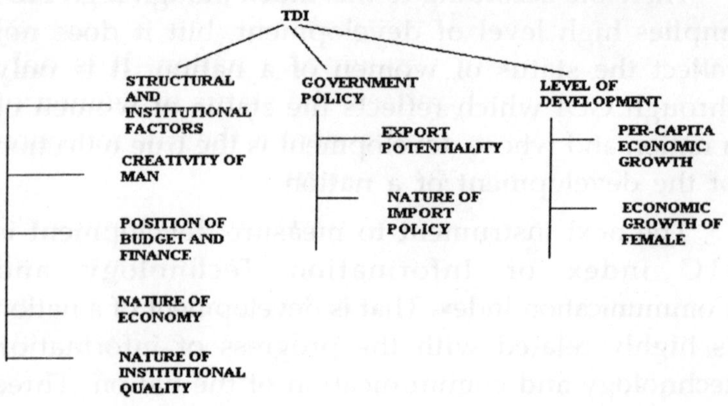

In the XI th Plan the new concept that is Inclusive Growth has been introduced.

A Development Policy Report (DPR) in 2006 by World Bank reveals that inclusive growth is the indisputable way to reform the regional imbalances and strengthen economic gains. The DPR report also reveals that the inclusive growth process should go towards the enhancement of the quality of basic services including education, power, healthcare and water supply for every individuals across the country.

The Indian economy, which has over the last six decades passed through various phases of growth, is now all set to enter an altogether different orbit: one marked by a high rate of expansion, combined with 'inclusive growth.' The term, inclusive growth, is finding its way increasingly in the lexicon of government leaders, economists, planners, academicians and businessmen, not just in India but even internationally. Robert Zoellick, president of the World Bank group, focused on the theme of 'An Inclusive and Sustainable Globalisation,' at a recent meet in Washington DC. "Globalization must not leave the 'bottom billion' behind," remarked the new chief of the World Bank. "This assertion is based on more than respect for the worth of our fellow men and women, and beyond an appreciation that any of us might have been born in similar circumstances. Inclusive globalization is also a matter of self-interest. Poverty breeds instability, disease, and devastation of common resources and the environment. Poverty can lead to broken societies that can become breeding grounds of those bent on destruction and to migrations that risk lives."

Thus the concept of inclusive growth is very broad and covers economic, social, and cultural aspects of development. In a simple language, 'Inclusive Growth' is a synonymous with 'equitable development' although it holds tremendous conceptual clarity about the idea of inclusiveness'. It implies an equitable allocation of resources with benefits accruing to every section of community.

Prof. H. Goswami and K.C. Borah define 'Inclusive growth ' is a process of development which generates opportunities for livelihood, provision for capacity building, easy access to basic amenities and sense of security against all kinds of threats in tandem with sustain and foster growth of GDP.'

According to A.K. Bezbaruah 'the term 'inclusive growth' is used interchangeably with broad based growth, pro poor growth and shared growth'. However inclusive growth is distinct by itself. A scheme or program whereby there is sustained poverty reduction through productive employment rather than direct income redistribution may be termed as a strategy for inclusive growth. it aims at increasing the income for the excluded groups. By excluded group he meant SCs, STs, OBCs and minorities.

According to P. Hazarica, there are various ways to define inclusive growth.

Firstly, it refer to holistic growth, an economic condition of a country where people even hailing from different countries can live in peace and progressive harmony and every one could march forward instead of plunging in perpetual war and anarchy.

Secondly, inclusive growth implies an ideal state of just and equitable allocation of resources which benefits accruing to every section of the society. Society is composed of a variety of people having distinct identity in terms of castes, creed, language, ethnicity, beliefs, attitude, dogma; but living together under a common law, common administration, and common economic plan and political frame work for well being of all and speedy development.

According to the third one it refers to rapid and continuous poverty reduction that allows people to contribute and benefit from economic growth for substantial poverty reduction rapid economic growth is a necessary condition. But, the growth to be substantial in the long-run, it should be broad based covering all sectors of the economy and all sections of the society and inclusive of largest proportion of countries labour force.

It implies growth with inclusion, such that the benefits of growth should reach to the vulnerable section of the society. In other words growth should be job added not jobless. This is nothing but the old wine in the new bottle.

Out of all these measure the most popular one is HDI. In our country almost all the states including eight northeastern states have joined the race in producing human development reports for their own states, some are already published few are yet to come. In this paper an attempt has been taken to investigate a comparative study regarding development of eight states in North-East India.

3.2 Data and Methodology

Datas are collected from various issues of RBI bulletin, CMIE, Central Statistical Organization (CSO), Economic Survey of India, Human Development Report of various states etc. As far as methodology is concerned simple growth rate, Average growth rate, diagrammatic representation of the data sets etc are used.

3.3 Objective of the Study

This paper is prepared on the basis of the availability of the data. Initially an attempt has been done to through some light on the concept of development, the next successive sections deals with the comparative situation of North-Eastern states with respect to various economic variables. Hence the main objective is to through some light on its present economic position compared to national average. Policy prescriptions are not done, since it is the birth-right of political leaders.

3.4 Some Birds' Eye View Regarding North-East States of India

Figure 3.2

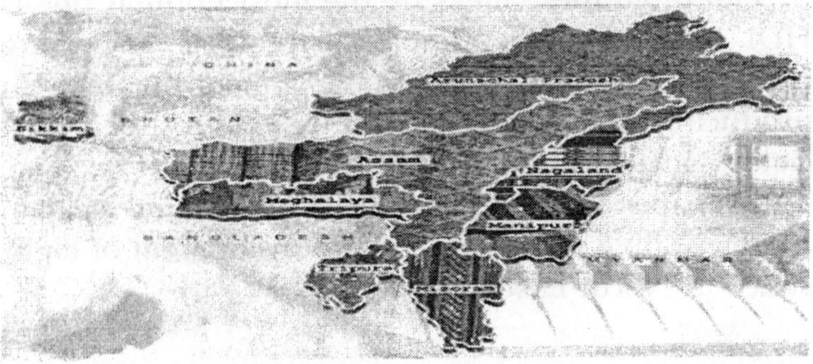

Source: Downloaded from the Google search 'Economy of North-East India'.

The North East region of India constitutes a land surface of 262230 square kilometers where a population of 38.9 million belonging to different ethnic groups inhabits. This region is a meeting place of large number of races, creeds, cultures and languages. Topographically the north-east region is a mixture of hills and plains. Sikkim, Nagaland, Mizoram, Meghalaya and Arunachal Pradesh are almost hilly, the rests have both plains and to some extent hills. Some important socio-economic indicators are given in the table below which may be treated as a bird's eye view about this region.

Table 3.1

States	*Population Growth (1991-2001)*	*Area (Sq.Km)*	*Literacy rate (2001)*		*HDI*		
			Male	*Female*	*1981*	*1991*	*2001*
India	22.7		75.8	54.2	0.263	0.381	0.56
Arunachal	27	83743 (B)	63.8 (L)	43.5 (L)	0.228 (L)	0.328 (L)	0.49 (L)
Assam	18.9	78483	71.3	54.6	0.261 (7th)	0.348 (7th)	0.50 (7th)
Manipur	17.9	22327	80.3	60.5	0.440 (H)	0.536 (2nd)	0.59 (3rd)
Meghalaya	30.7	22429	65.4	59.6	0.293 (5th)	0.365 (6th)	0.52 (5th)
Mizoram	28.8	21081	90.7 (H)	86.7 (H)	0.381 (2nd)	0.548 (H)	0.67 (H)

Nagaland	64.5	16579	71.5	61.5	0.295	0.486	0.57
	(H)				(4th)	(3rd)	(4th)
Tripura	16	10492	81.0	64.9	0.264	0.389	0.59
	(L)	•			(6th)	(5th)	(3rd)
Sikkim	33.1	7096	76	60.4	0.302	0.425	0.60
	(S)				(3rd)	(4th)	(2nd)

Source: National HDR, 2001, Planning Commission, New Delhi.

Figure 3.3

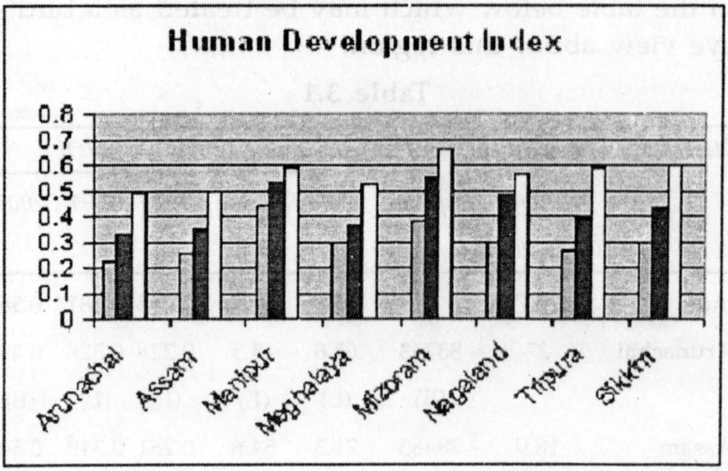

Source: Tripura and Assam Human Development Report

3.5 Findings

With respect to area Arunachal Pradesh is biggest state among eight north-east states, the second largest is Assam, where as the smallest one is Tripura. The 1st column of Table-1 shows with respect to decadal growth of population Nagaland is the highest with 6.45 percent increase per year during last ten years (1991-2001) while Tripura is again lowest with 1.6% growth of population during the same period of time.

With respect to literacy rate the highest literacy is in Mizoram both male and female with 90.7% and 86.7% respectively in 2001, whereas Arunachal Pradesh is lowest with 63.8 and 43.5 % male and female literacy respectively. The last three columns show the Human Development Index in three decades, (1981, 1991, and 2001) which shows Mizoram is the most developed states among north-east states and it maintains its rank for last twenty years. On the other hand Arunachal Pradesh is the most underdeveloped states among the eight north-east states in India. Sikkim and Tripura shows the improvement of rank with respect to HDI, other states are more or less maintaining the same level of status.Figure-2 shows that though all the states are improving with respect to the absolute value of HDI, but the rate of improvement is different. Since Human Development Index consists of three different indices that is income index, health index and education index, next section deals with the comparative situation of health and education.

Figure 3.4

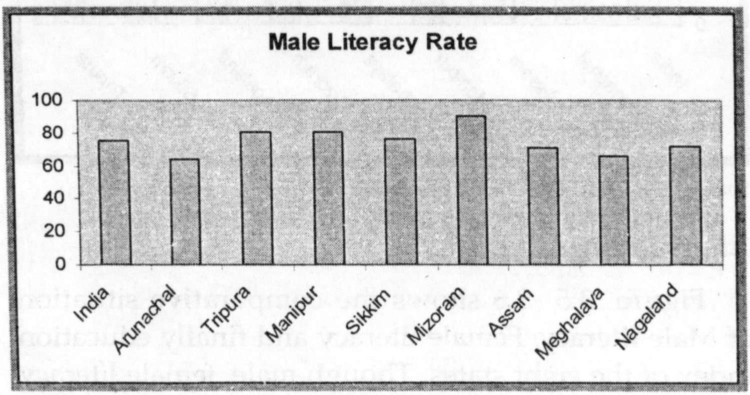

Source: self computed from the data (2000-01)

Figure 3.5

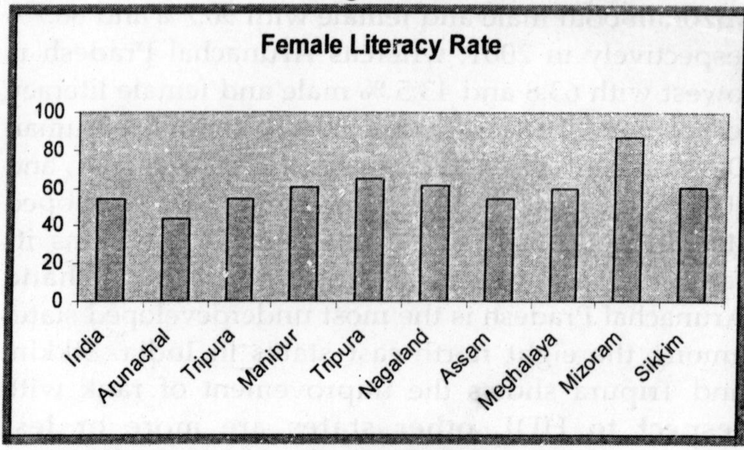

Source: self computed from the data (2000-01)

Figure 3.6

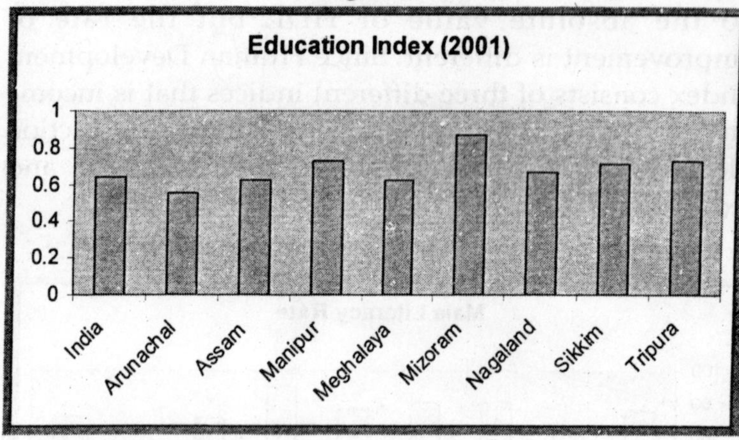

Source: self computed from the data (2000-01)

3.5.1 Findings

Figure 3.5 -3.6 shows the comparative situation of Male literacy, Female literacy and finally education index of the eight states. Though male, female literacy is one of the important ingredients of education index but there are some other elements for example drop-out rate, gross enrollment, adult literacy etc. which also play a vital role in forming this index.

Figure 3.7

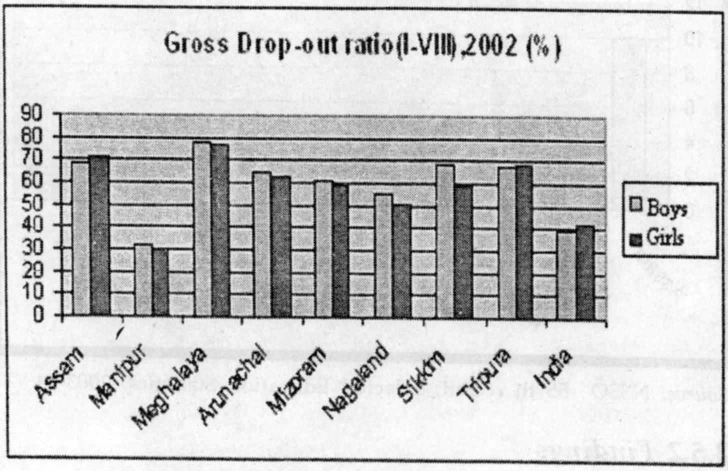

Source: Annual Report 2003-04, Ministry of Human Resource Development

Figure 3.8

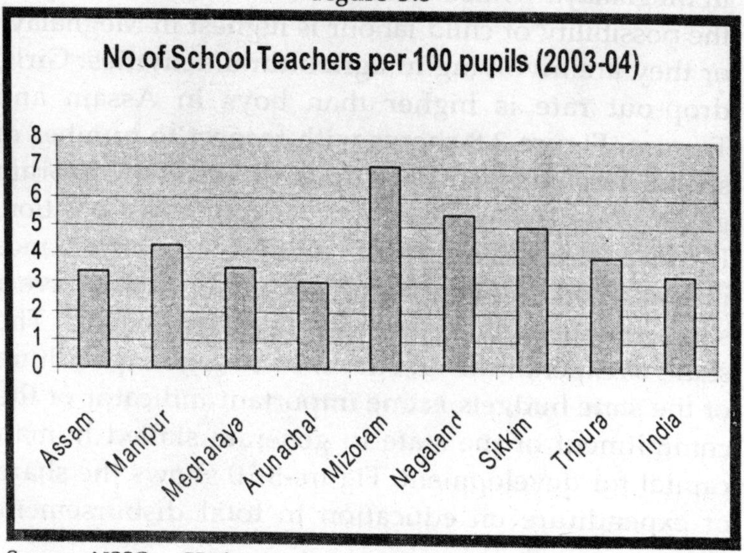

Source: NSSO 55 th round, Selected Education Statistics, 2003-04.

Figure 3.9

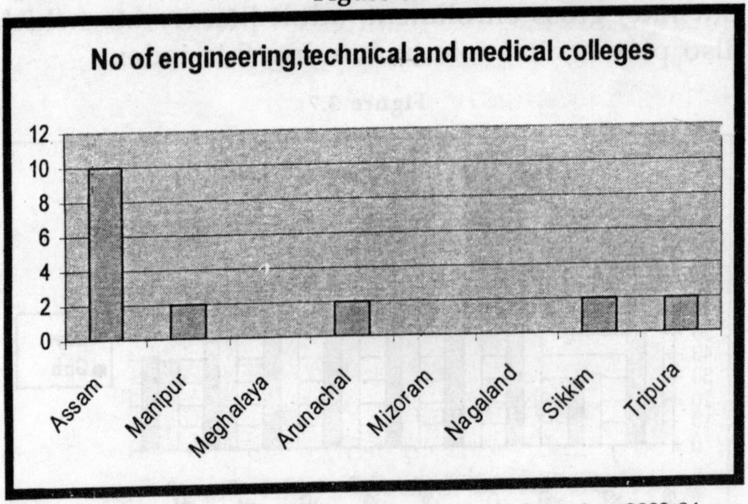

Source: NSSO 55 th round, Selected Education Statistics, 2003-04

3.5.2 *Findings*

Figure-3.7 shows that drop-out rates are highest in Meghalaya while in Manipur it is lowest. It implies the possibility of child labour is highest in Meghalaya or they are involving in agricultural activities. Girls' drop-out rate is higher than boys in Assam and Tripura. Figure-3.8 shows with respect to number of school teachers per 100 pupils in 2003-04 Mizoram got the top place while Arunachal got the last position. Figure-3.9 shows inspite of having good performance in education, Mizoram, and Nagaland do not have a single engineering or medical college in 2002-03. The share of expenditure on education in total expenditure of the state budgets is one important indicator of the commitment of the state to generate skilled human capital for development. Figure-3.10 shows the share of expenditure on education to total disbursement (%).

Figure 3.10

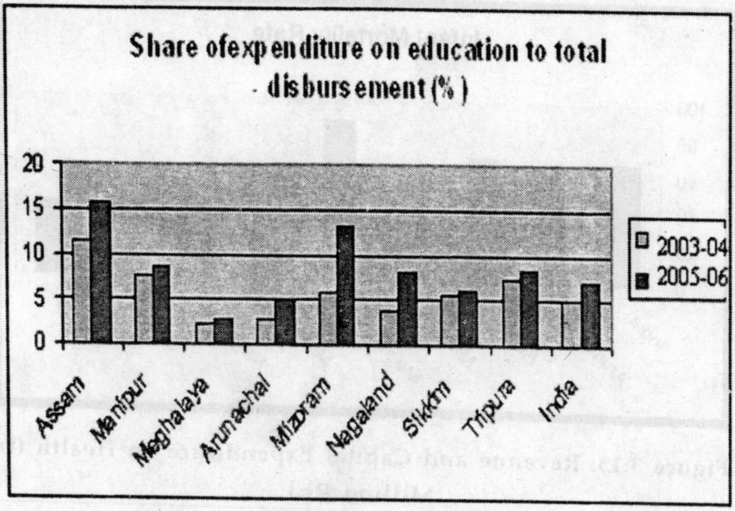

Source: RBI, Budget documents of State Governments.

From the above Figure (3.10) it is clear that government of Assam is spending highest on education, on the other hand Government of Meghalaya is spending lowest on education in terms of their total expenditure percentage among the north-eastern states in India.

Figure 3.11

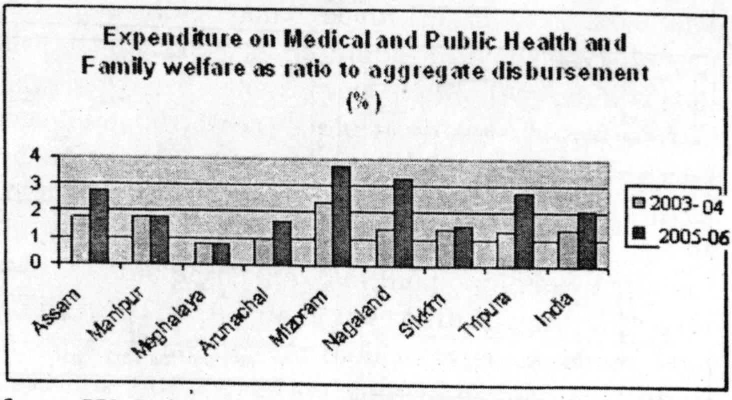

Source: RBI, Budget documents of State Governments

Figure 3.12

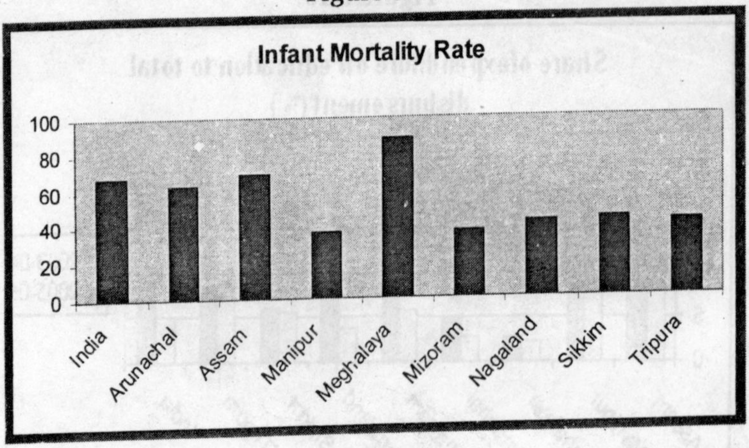

Figure 3.13: Revenue and Capital Expenditure on Health (In Million Rs.)

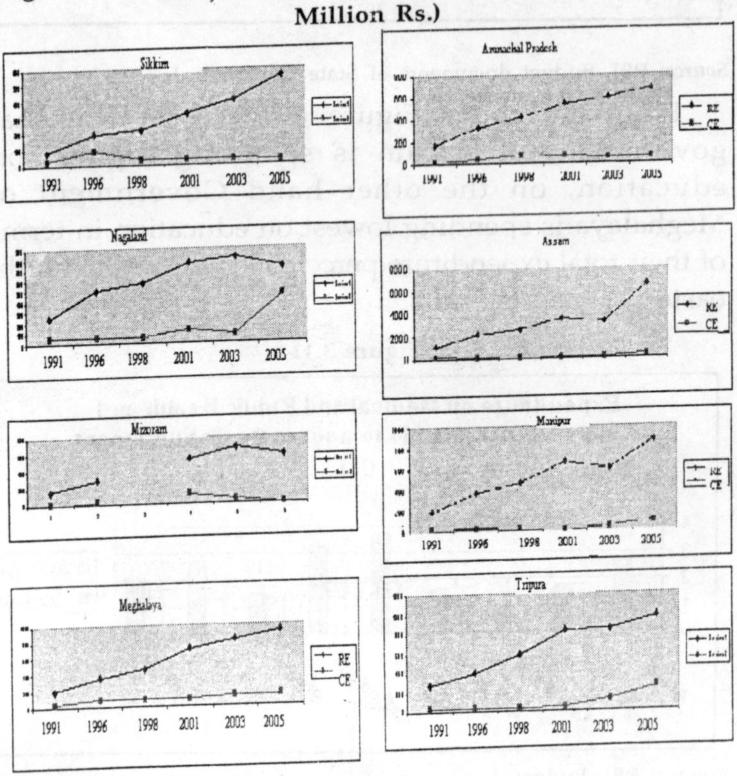

Source: Upto 1987 Finance and Revenue Accounts Comptroller and Auditor General of India , GOI ,respective year, 2001 RBI,2003,2005 public finance CMIE 2005

Figure 3.14

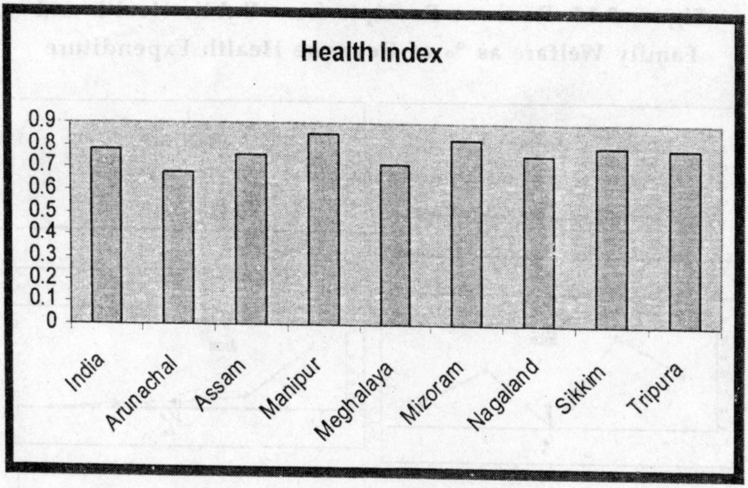

Source: Tripura Human Development Report (2003)

3.5.3 *Findings*

Figure 3.11-3.14 deals with health indices of the north east states. Figure-3.11 shows that Mizoram is spending highest in public health and family welfare in 2005-06, where as Meghalaya is spending lowest in terms of % of total disbursement. Figure-3.12 shows infant mortality rate is highest in Meghalaya where as it is lowest in Manipur. Figure-3.13 shows the revenue and capital expenditure of the N-E states of India on health. It shows that though revenue expenditure increases for all the states, where as capital expenditure on health are more or less fixed , only in Tripura and Nagaland, and Manipur it increases little bit. Figure-3.14 deals with health indices for the year 2003, which shows Manipur got the highest place with respect to health index. One interesting thing is that except Arunachal Pradesh and Meghalaya all other states in north-east are above the national average with respect to health index.

Figure 3.15: Revenue Receipts from Public Health and Family Welfare as % of Revenue Health Expenditure

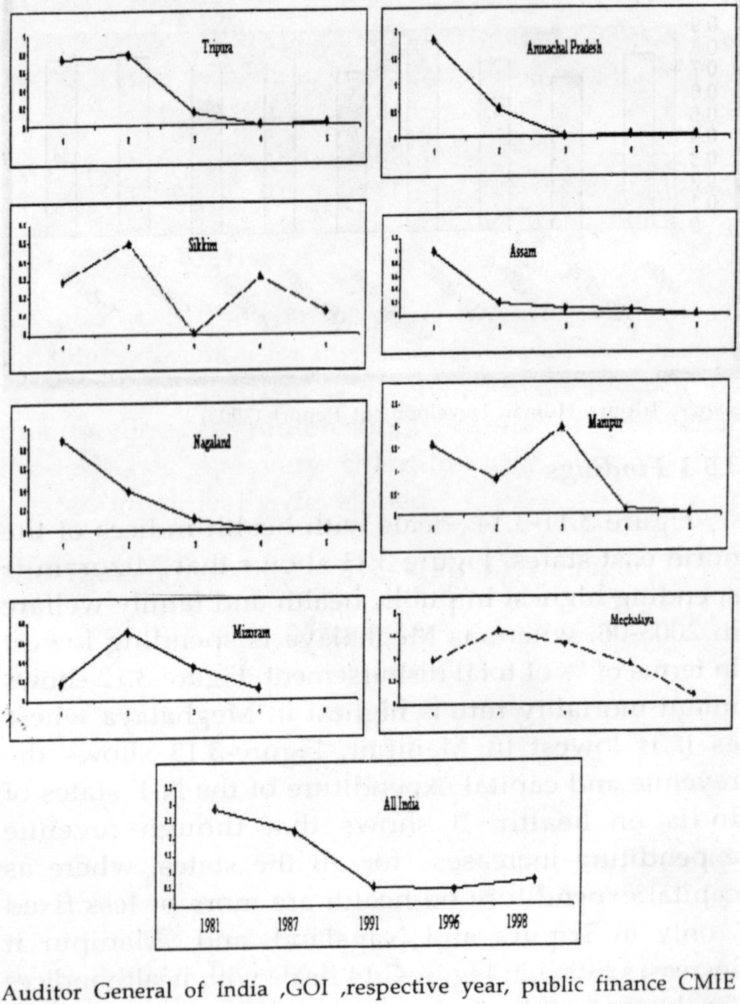

Auditor General of India ,GOI ,respective year, public finance CMIE 2004

Figure-3.15 shows the revenue receipts from public health and Family welfare as % of Revenue health expenditure is declining for all the states except Sikkim, in Sikkim it is fluctuating, where as for national average it has an upward trend.

Figure 3.16: A Comparison of NSDP Growth between North East States and Delhi

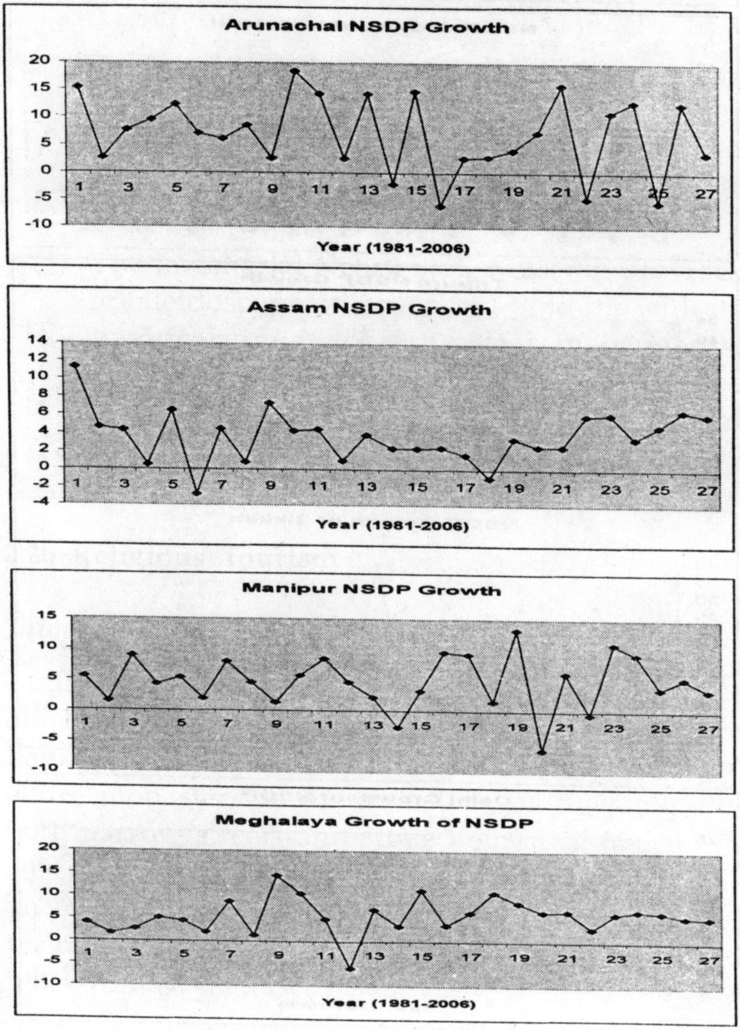

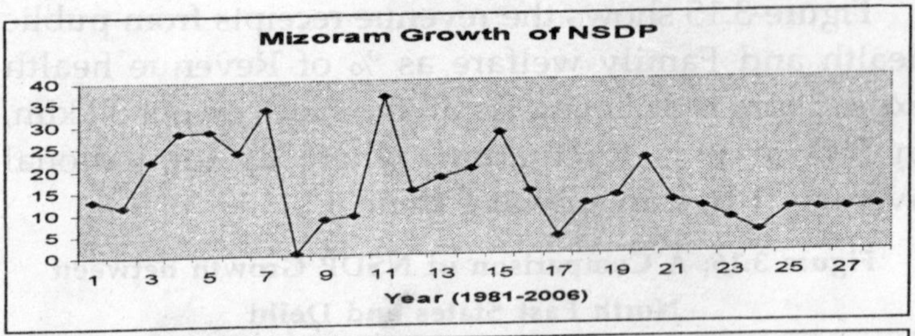
Mizoram Growth of NSDP
Year (1981-2006)

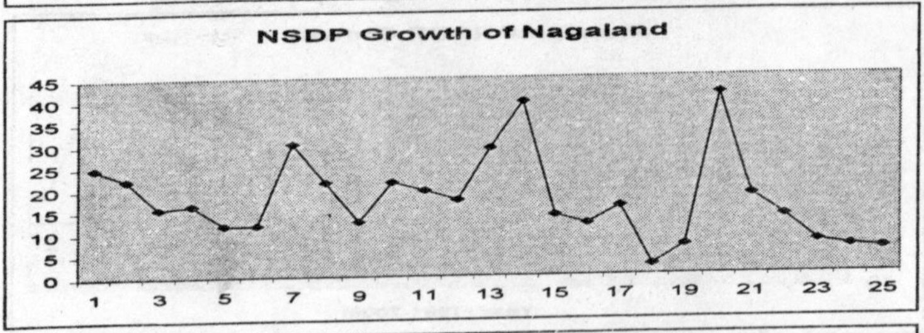
NSDP Growth of Nagaland

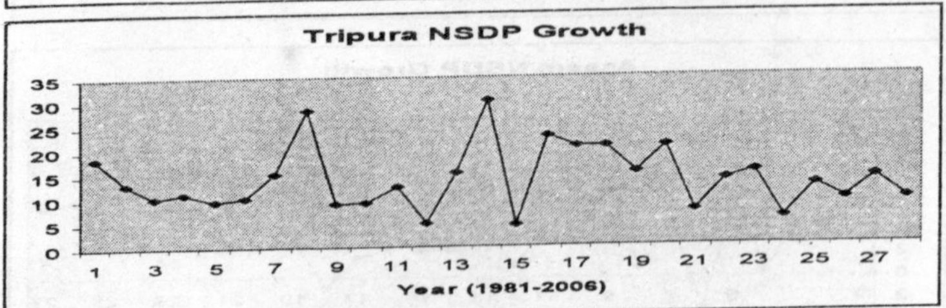
Tripura NSDP Growth
Year (1981-2006)

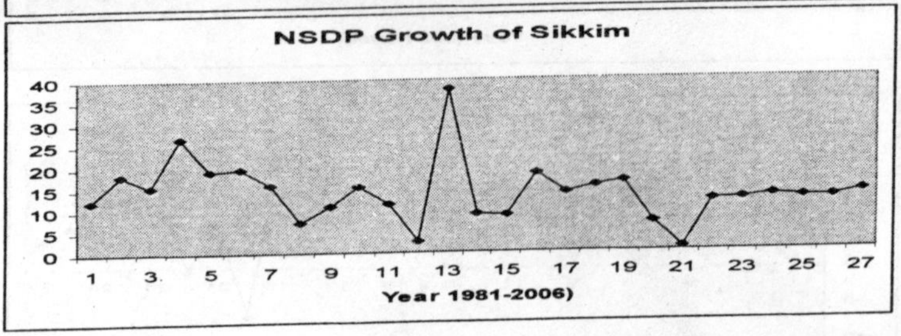
NSDP Growth of Sikkim
Year 1981-2006)

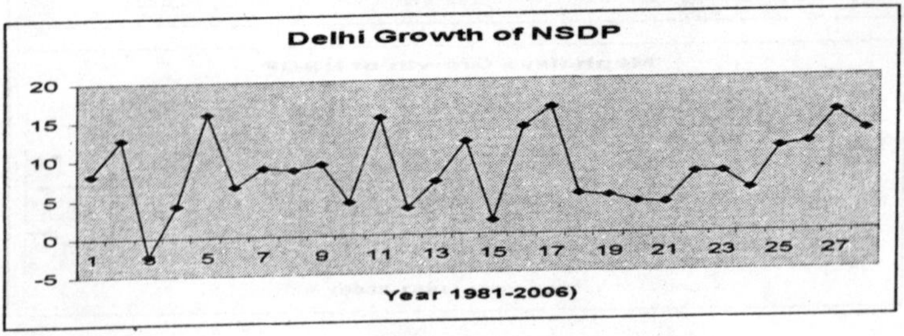
Delhi Growth of NSDP
Year 1981-2006)

Figure-3.16 shows the Growth of Net State Domestic Product (NSDP) of all the NE states and Delhi. From this figure it is clear that there is an upward trend in the growth rate of NSDP in Delhi, where as in Sikkim after a certain fluctuation from 1981-1992 it has a huge increase but side by side a corresponding decrease in the nest year ,but after 2000 it has a stable growth rate .Assam shows a slowly increasing trend , where as Arunachal, Manipur and Meghalaya's growth pattern is not stable it is fluctuating in nature. In Mizoram also it has an upward trend.

Figure 3.17: (Per-Capita NSDP Comparison with National Average)

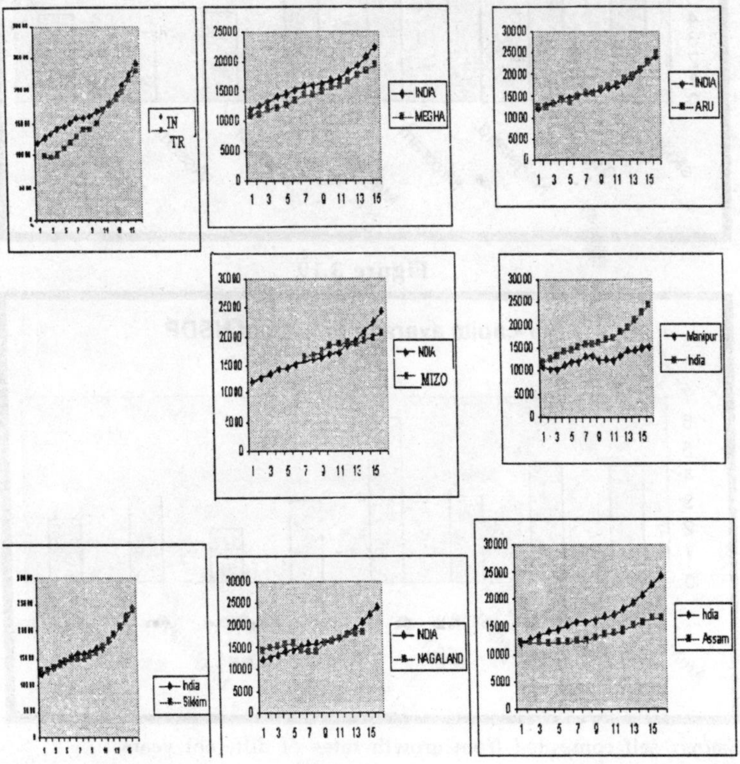

Figure 3.17 shows a comparison of per-capita NSDP with national average. Which shows Assam and Manipur are much below the national average with respect to per-capita income, where as Sikkim, Arunachal and Tripura are more or less moving at the same rate of national average, for Mizoram some times it exceeds national average, but last couple of years it is going below the national average.

Figure 3.18

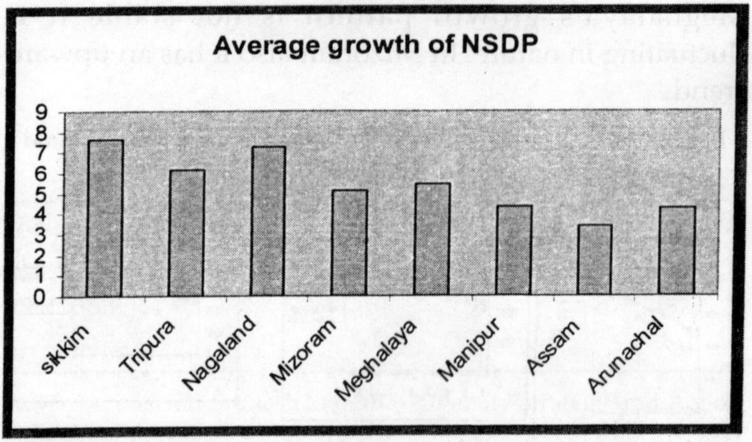

Figure 3.19

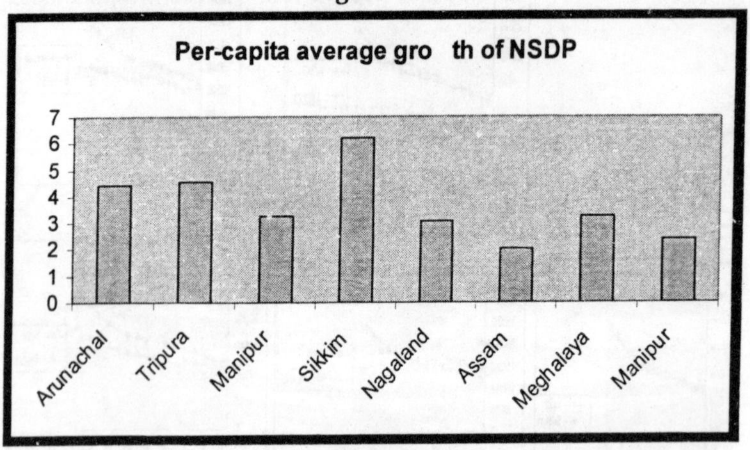

Source: self computed from growth rates of different years

3.5.4 Findings:

Figure- 3.18-3.19 shows average growth of NSDP and average growth of per-capita NSDP , from which it is clear that with respect to both the indicators Sikkim stood at the top place, where as Assam is in lowest place. Therefore with respect to income it can be said Assam is the poorest state among the all North-East states in India.

Figure 3.20

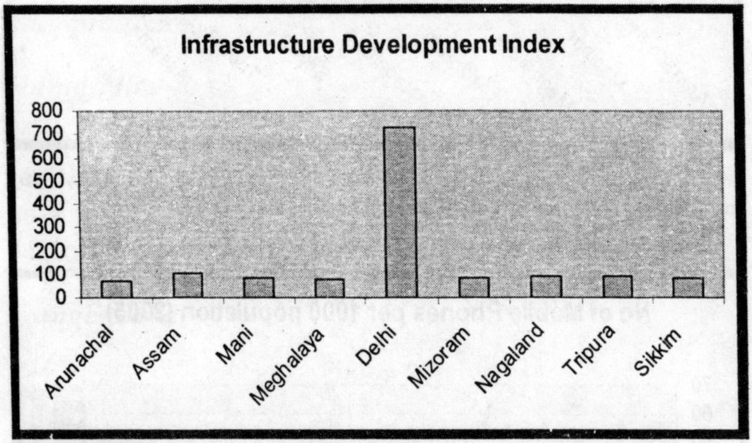

Source: CMIE

Figure 3.21

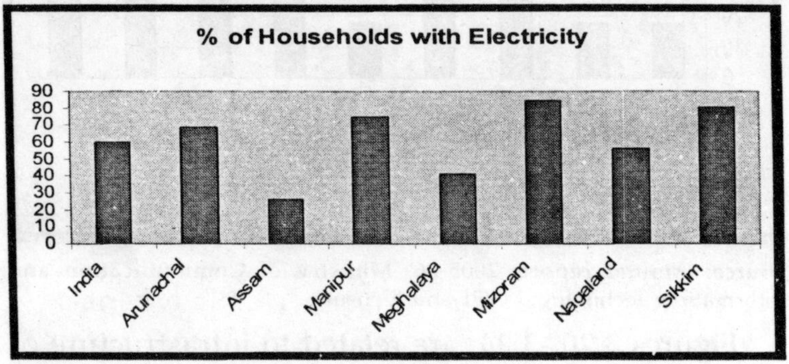

Source: International Institute for Population Sciences, Mumbai, India (2000), National Family Health Survey (1998-99)

Figure 3.22

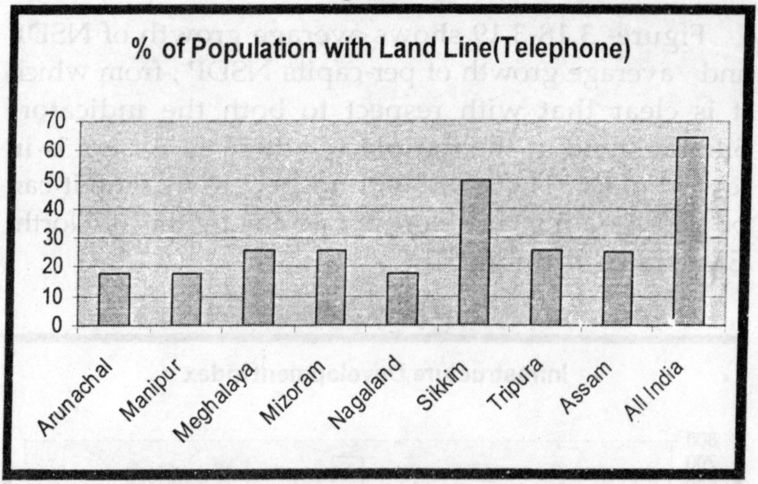

Source: Annual report 2002-03, Ministry of Communication and Information Technology, GOI and Census.

Figure 3.23

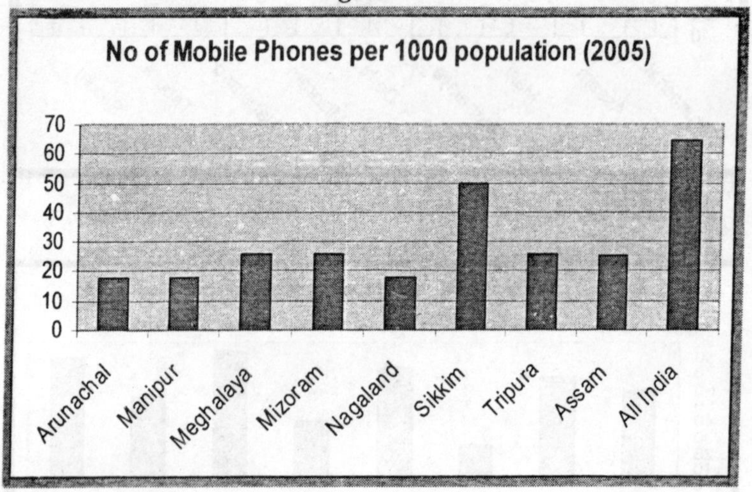

Source: Annual report, 2005-06, Ministry of Communication and Information Technology, GOI and Census

Figures 3.20 -3.23 are related to infrastructure of the north-east states. Figure-3.20 shows with respect to Infrastructure Development Index all the eight north-eastern states are more or less at the same situation, but when we compare it with respect to Delhi it is easy to understand the infrastructural difference between these two regions. With respect to households with electricity, Mizoram got highest place where as in Assam, % of households with electricity connection is lowest.

Today communication modes like telephones and cellular phones are very essential for connecting various parts of the country with each other and with the rest of the world. Telephone is easily accessible and cheaper mode of communication and the density of telephones is an indicator of the level of development and potential for growth in a state. Similarly mobile phone technology is rapidly becoming a necessity even in rural areas also. This has increased the efficiency, moreover a higher penetration of mobile phonies the reflection of growing acceptance of a technology which helps in development process. Figure-3.23 shows with respect to use of mobile phone Sikkim got the highest place among north-east states. But all the eight states are much below the national average both in terms of land line and mobile phone.

Figure 3.24

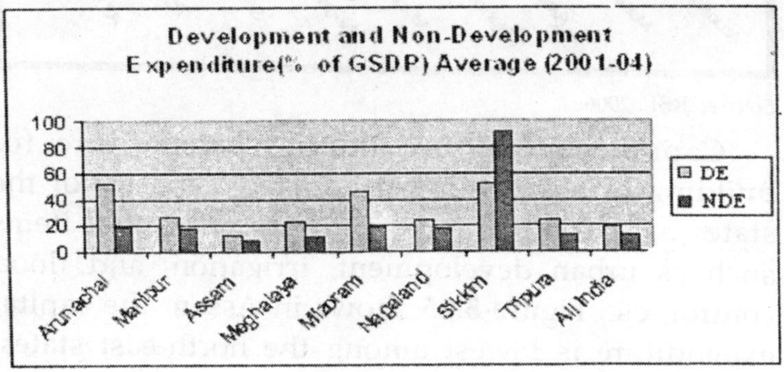

Source: RBI,2006.

Development expenditure should form the core of the expenditure in states with low levels of social and infrastructural development. This includes social sector spending on health and education, expenditure on poverty alleviation programmes, irrigation systems etc. These expenditures are very essential for states to focus on these areas to build up capacity within state to generate more income and higher growth. On the hand non-development expenditure comprises expenditure on subsidies, interest payments, salaries and pensions etc. The rising share of this kind of committed spending was a cause of concern and all the states are directed by centre to curtail such expenditure. Figure-3.24 shows only in Sikkim non-development expenditure are greater than development expenditure in terms of % of GSDP.

Figure 3.25

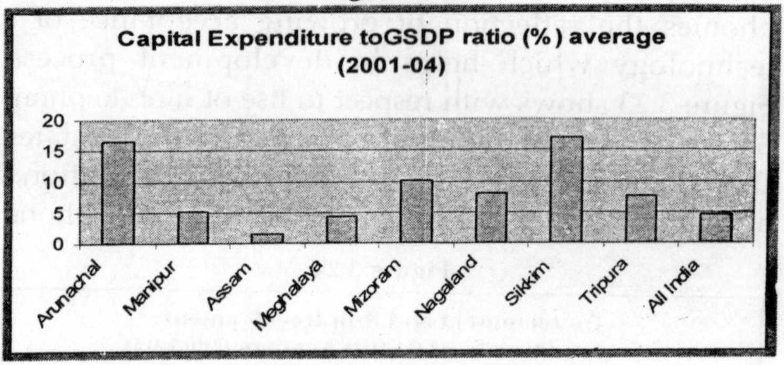

Source: RBI, 2006.

Capital expenditure implies expenditure for building or augmenting productive capacity of the states as it comprises expenditure on capital items such as urban development, irrigation, and flood control, etc. Figure-3.25 shows in Assam the capital expenditure is lowest among the north-east states, where as it is highest in Sikkim.

The interest payments to revenue receipts ratio is crucial to determine the extent to which the state can cover the cost of interest payments in a year by the revenue receipts earned that year. This is an excellent indicator of the ability of a state to live within its means, as a lower ratio shows that the state can provide for other running expenditure with the revenue earned. On the other hand higher ratio means the states have little to run expenditure after paying interest. The Figure-3.26 below shows the interest payments to revenue receipts ratio (in terms of %) of the NE states, which tells that Government of Assam is paying highest for interest payment among the eight north-east states, where as government of Sikkim is paying minimum in this respect.

Figure 3.26

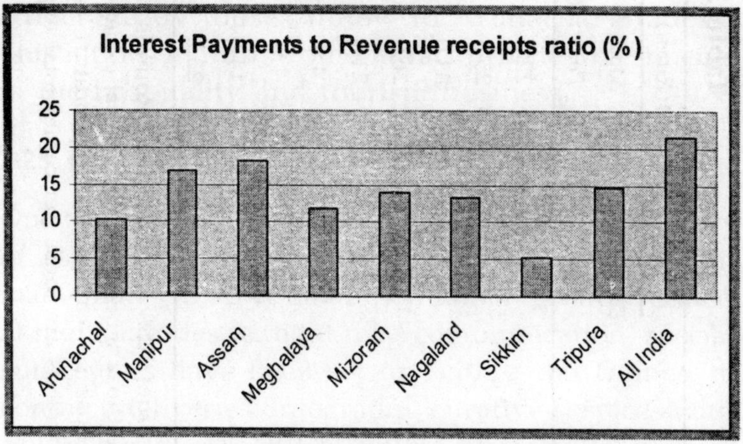

Table 3.2-3.3 show the incidence of Poverty in 1993-94 and 1999-2000, in terms of percentage in rural and urban respectively.

Table 3.2

State	*1993-94(Rural)*				*1999-2000 (Rural)*			
	Extreme poor	*Very poor*	*Mod. Poor*	*Poor (below BPL)*	*Extreme poor*	*Very poor*	*Mod. Poor*	*Poor (below BPL)*
India	2.0	14.7	22.1	36.8	0.8	8.2	18.3	26.5
Arunachal	2.5	16.1	25.3	41.4	0.0	6.3	17.1	23.4
Assam	0.7	12.3	33.0	45.3	1.9	14.8	25.4	40.2
Manipur	0.1	2.3	16.9	19.2	0.0	2.4	11.7	14.1
Meghalaya	0.2	2.9	21.4	24.3	0.0	0.2	5.8	6.0
Mizoram	0.0	1.3	4.9	6.2	0.0	0.1	2.7	2.8
Nagaland	0.0	0.0	1.9	1.9	0.0	0.0	0.2	0.2
Tripura	0.9	8.7	14.6	23.3	0.2	3.2	13.5	16.7
Sikkim	0.0	8.1	23.2	31.3	0.2	3.2	18.5	21.7

Source: Computed from NSS 50th and 55th Rounds data on Household Consumer expenditure, where Extremely poor are those whose per capita total expenditure is less than 50% of the state-specific poverty line, Very poor whose per-capita total expenditure is less than 75% of the state-specific poverty line, Moderately poor persons are those per-capita total expenditure lies between 75 to 100% of state specific poverty lines.

Table 3.3

State	*1993-94(Urban)*				*1999-2000 (Urban)*			
	Extreme poor	*Very poor*	*Mod. Poor*	*Poor (below BPL)*	*Extreme poor*	*Very poor*	*Mod. Poor*	*Poor (below BPL)*
India	2.9	15.1	17.7	32.8	1.2	9.2	14.8	24
Arunachal	0.4	1.9	3.9	5.8	2.2	4.1	0.9	5.0
Assam	0.2	1.2	6.8	8.0	0.2	2.1	5.1	7.2
Manipur	0.2	0.4	6.5	6.9	0.0	0.0	0.5	0.5
Meghalaya	0.0	0.1	1.7	1.8	0.0	0.0	0.0	0.0
Mizoram	0.0	0.0	0.0	0.0	0.0	0.0	0.0	0.0
Nagaland	0.0	0.0	0.0	0.0	0.0	0.0	0.0	0.0
Tripura	0.1	1.8	4.2	6.0	0.0	0.4	1.0	1.4
Sikkim	0.0	0.0	1.0	1.0	0.0	1.2	3.6	4.8

Source: Computed from NSS 50th and 55th Rounds data on Household Consumer expenditure, where Extremely poor are those whose per capita total expenditure is less than 50% of the state-specific poverty line, Very poor whose per-capita total expenditure is less than 75% of the state-specific poverty line, Moderately poor persons are those per-capita total expenditure lies between 75 to 100% of state specific poverty lines.

3.6 Findings

From the above table it is clear in rural areas Arunachal did well in reducing extreme, very, moderate and poor ,where as in Assam percentage of extreme and very poor increased, in this respect the significant improvement in reducing poverty occurs in Nagaland, Mizoram, and Meghalaya. Table-3.3 shows in urban areas there is no such type of poverty in Mizoram, Nagaland and Meghalaya, where as it has increased in Sikkim.

Figure-3.27 shows the change in sectoral share of GSDP of eight north-east states and that of the national average. From this figure it is clear that only in Nagaland the share of primary sector has increased and that of in the secondary and tertiary sector has decreased where as in Mizoram share of industry and in Tripura share of tertiary has decreased little bit during the time period (1999-2005). On the other hand rest of the states follow the national average pattern which indicates the path of development in the traditional sense.

Figure 3.27: Sectoral Composition of GSDP

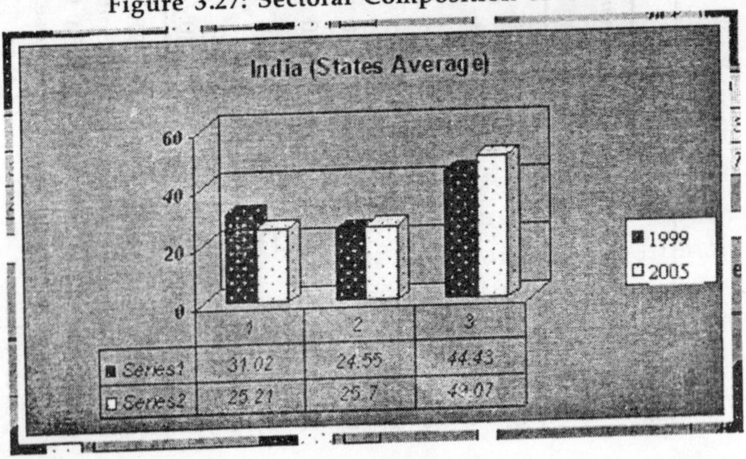

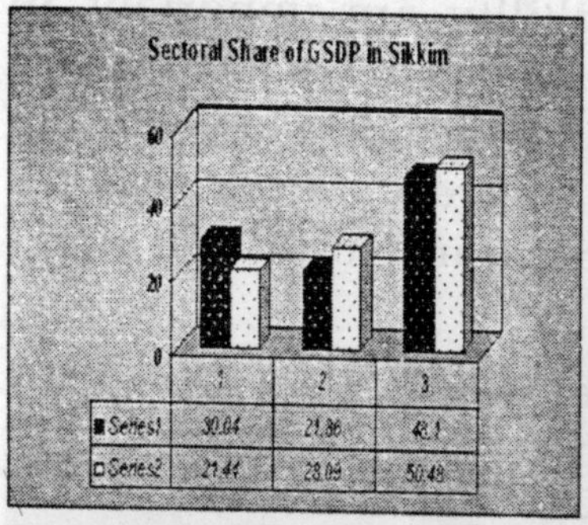
Sectoral Share of GSDP in Sikkim
60
40
20
0
1
2
3
Series1 30.04 21.86 48.1
Series2 21.44 28.09 50.48

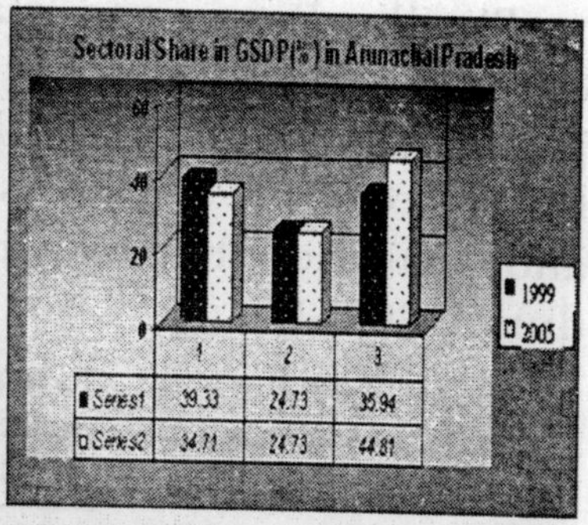
Sectoral Share in GSDP(%) in Arunachal Pradesh
60
40
20
0
1
2
3
Series1 39.33 24.73 35.94
Series2 34.71 24.73 44.81
1999
2005

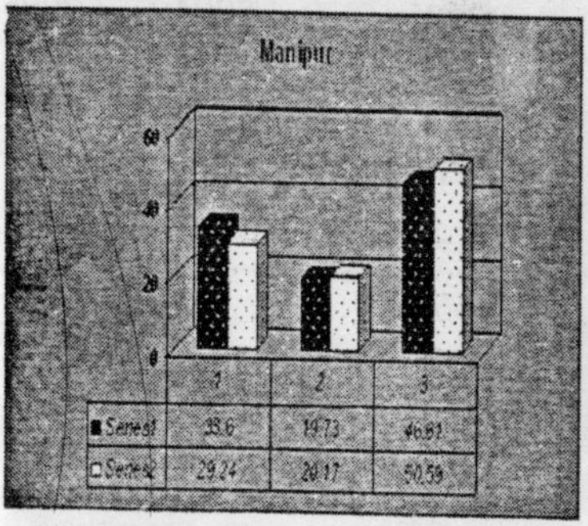
Manipur
60
40
20
0
1
2
3
Series1 35.6 19.73 46.81
Series2 29.24 20.17 50.59

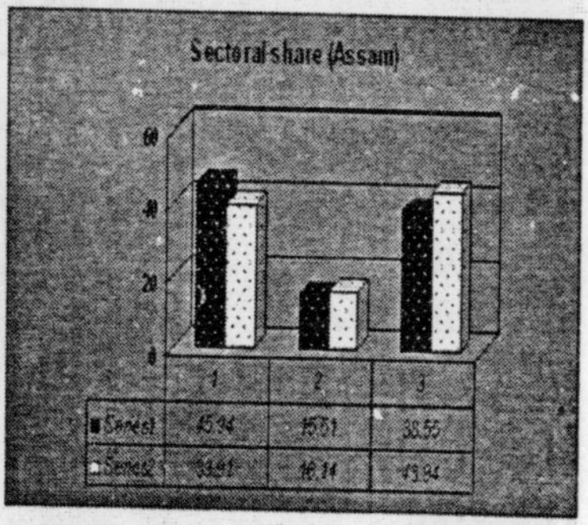
Sectoral share (Assam)
60
40
20
0
1
2
3
Series1 45.94 15.51 38.55
Series2 16.14 43.94

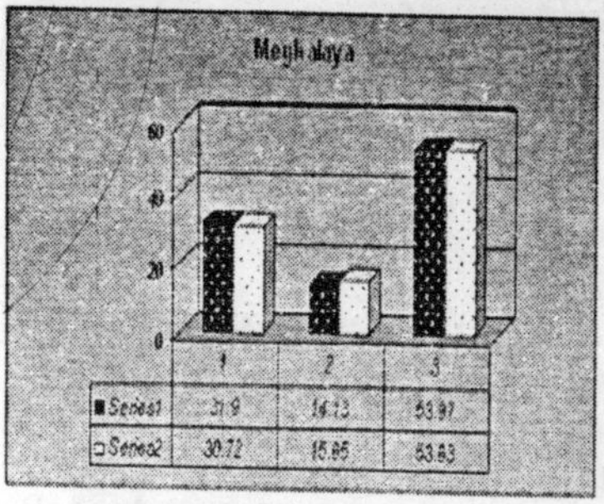
Meghalaya
60
40
20
0
1
2
3
Series1 31.9 14.13 53.97
Series2 30.72 15.65 53.63

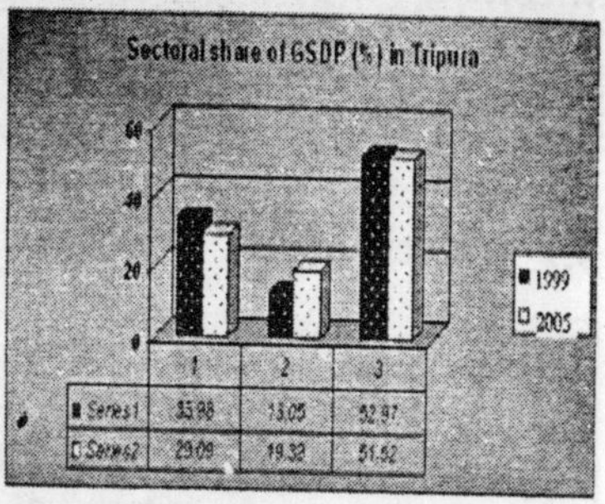
Sectoral share of GSDP (%) in Tripura
60
40
20
0
1
2
3
Series1 33.98 13.05 52.97
Series2 29.09 19.32 51.52
1999
2005

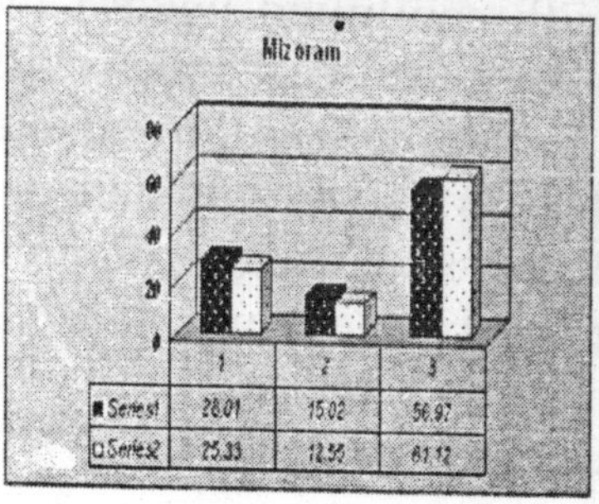
Mizoram
80
60
40
20
0
1
2
3
Series1 28.01 15.02 56.97
Series2 25.33 12.55 61.12

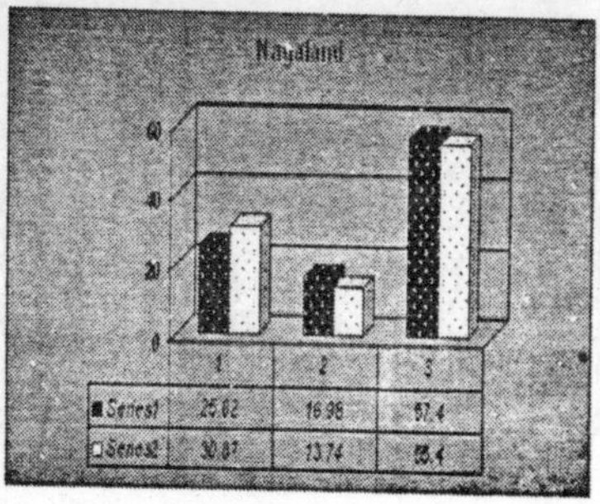
Nagaland
60
40
20
0
1
2
3
Series1 25.62 16.98 57.4
Series2 30.87 13.74 55.4

Finally, Peace and stability are important to complement and support good governance, which promotes an environment in which development can take place. Table-3.4 shows different violent incidents and casualties that took place in North-East states during 2004-05.

Table 3.4

States	*Violent Incidents*		*Civilians killed*	
	2004	*2005*	*2004*	*2005*
Assam	267	398	194	173
Tripura	212	115	67	28
Nagaland	186	192	42	28
Manipur	478	554	88	158
Meghalaya	47	37	17	1
Arunachal	41	32	6	3
Mizoram	3	4	-	2

Source: Government of India, Ministry of Home affairs, Annual Report, 2005, 2006.

3.7 Conclusion

There are lots of reasons for the backwardness of the north-east India. Some are historical, some are socio-economic and some are political. All these circumstances combined with continued neglect by different governments have left north-east states with a very weak infrastructure and limited and unreliable connectivity among themselves as well as with nations. This becomes a major obstacle to socio-economic development. On the other hand violent and divisive conflict triggered by armed insurgent groups directly affecting human security by bringing fear and death of civilians at every moments. If these problems especially in terms of infrastructure, income growth and overall development is not properly addressed, one day this region may fall into the trap of vicious quadrant rather than to a virtuous one. There have been lots of discussions, regarding these problems of North-East India since long, but the time has come for the real big push by all the governments in this neglected segments of India.

REFERENCES

Arunachal Pradesh Human Development Report, 2003.

Assam Human Development Report, 2003.

Centre for Monitoring Indian Economy's Published Data (Down Load).

India Development Report, 2005.

Nayak Purusottam. *'Human Development Reports on North-East India: A Bird's Eye View'*: (Down Load).

National Human Development Report, 2001.

Radhakrishna R., and Ray Shovan: *'Poverty in India-Dimensions and Character'*- India Development Report, 2004-05.

Reserve Bank of India Bulletin.

Sikkim Human Development Report, 2001.

Todaro M.P. and Smith S.C. *Economic Development,* Eight editions, 2003.

Tripura Human Development Report, 2003.

4

Degree of Association between Forestry and Fishing in North–East India

4.1 Introduction

Man's dependence on forests for their livelihood and for raising the quality of life is age-old and this dependence continues even today. The importance of forestry in macro economic analysis has gained momentum after the Stockholm conference in seventies and Rio Summit of Nineties. As a matter of fact, forests have been playing a pivotal role in socio-economic development of our country in general and North East region in particular. It also plays an important role in containing the ecology of north-eastern region. Moreover, forests are important source of subsistence, employment, revenue and raw materials for industry.

In many countries economic welfare has historically been influenced by natural resources such as forests, in view of the fact, forests provide benefits that include environmental amelioration, water and soil conservation, fodder, and outdoor recreation. It also provides food, fuel, fibre, timber and many other non timber forest products.

Table below shows the area covered by forests (1999) in North-East India.

Table 4.1

States	*Areas (sq.km.)*	*% of total area*
Arunachal Pradesh	68,847	82.01
Assam	23,688	33.20
Manipur	17384	80
Meghalaya	15,633	69.80
Mizoram	18338	86.20
Nagaland	14164	86.90
Tripura	5745	50.90

Source: SFR, 1999

4.2 Objective of the Study

In this paper an attempt has been taken to investigate into the contributions of forestry and fishing to Net State Domestic Products (NSDP) of seven North-East states in India and the degree of association of such contributions across different states concerned.

4.3 Data

RBI data have been used and the time period of study ranges from 1999 to 2007. The variables are log NSDP, while the contribution of forestry and fisheries are being captured as % of NSDP.

4.4 Methodology

The study involves the use of Least Square Regression Method. The estimated linear regression equations with contributions of fisheries or forestry as regressor are considered. The coefficients are used to set up the t-difference matrices, where t-difference = difference in the estimated coefficients divided by the standard error of the estimates that is

t-difference = $\frac{\hat{\beta}_i - \hat{\beta}_j}{SE\ (\hat{\beta}_i - \hat{\beta}_j)}$ where SE= Standard Error of the estimate

Table 4.2: Comparative Situation of Forestry and Fishing (At Constant Prices)

States	*Arunachal*	*Assam*	*Manipur*	*Megha*	*Mizoram*	*Nagaland*	*Tripura*
NSDP(1999)	1497	32011	2954	3211	1410	2556	4496
NSDP(2007)	2452	46433	4000	5060	2205	4566	7889
Forestry(1999)	67.7	457.6	53.1	41.8	14	90	56.1
Forestry(2007)	59.2	448.6	74.8	63.3	23.2	139.3	63.8
Fishing(1999)	13.3	515.3	62.3	20.1	14.6	20.7	50.5
Fishing(2007)	13.9	563.8	59.5	26.7	17.3	20.7	87.1

4.5 Graphical Presentation

Figure 4.1

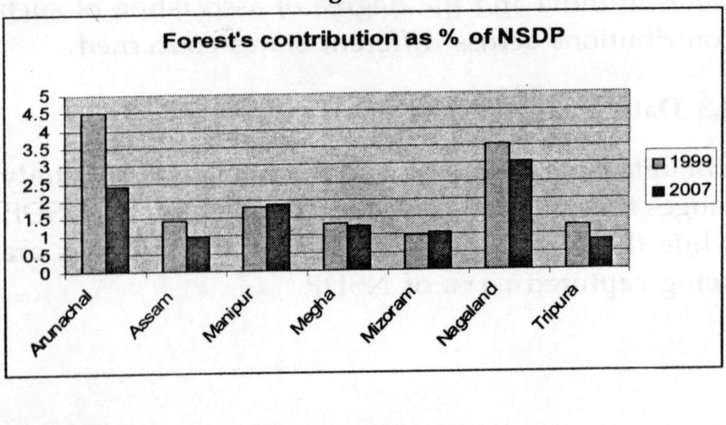

Figure 4.2

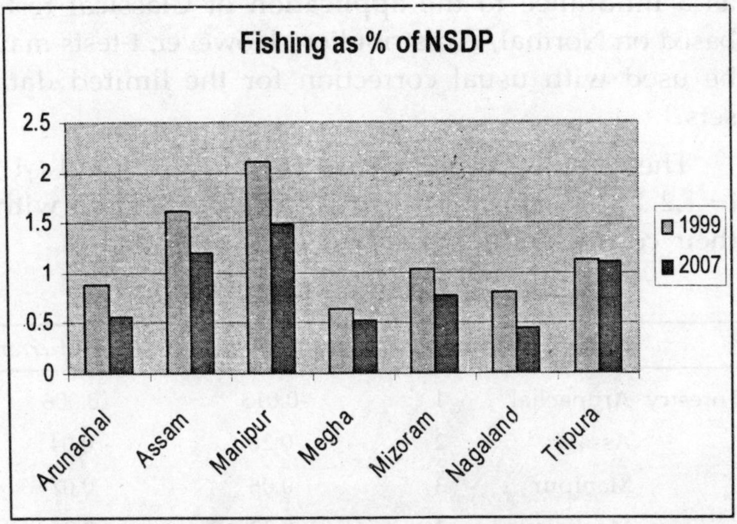

Figure-4.1 and 4.2 clearly shows that in all the states the contribution of forests declined from 1999 to 2007 almost all NE states except Manipur .On the other hand fishing is also depicting the same pattern. It implies a declining trend of the contribution of primary sector in NSDP.

4.6 Model

The model estimated for the study is basically of the following form

$\log NSDP = \alpha + \beta_i Forestry + \gamma_i Fishing + \mu_i$, where i = 1…7

This equation has been has been estimated for each of the seven N.E. States. Thus we have of estimated regression equation. The estimation suffers from the limitation of annual data and, therefore, the degree of freedom in such estimated equation is very low (df=5).

Such low degrees of freedom in estimation works as a hindrance to the application of Classical tests based on Normal/Z distribution. However, t-tests may be used with usual correction for the limited data sets.

The estimated coefficients ($\hat{\beta}$i, i=1,2,..7) and (γi , i= 1,2..7) have been presented in Table-3, along with their corresponding standard error statistics.

Table 4.3: Results of Estimation

	States	*Parameter*	*Estimated coefficient*	*Standard error*
Forestry	Arunachal	1	-0.013	0.006
	Assam	2	-0.28	0.04
	Manipur	3	-0.06	0.07
	Meghalaya	4	-0.22	0.26
	Mizoram	5	-0.49	0.07
	Nagaland	6	-0.02	0.05
	Tripura	7	-0.53	0.02
Fishing	Arunachal	1	-0.570	0.06
	Assam	2	-0.04	0.05
	Manipur	3	-0.19	0.02
	Meghalaya	4	-0.53	0.21
	Mizoram	5	-0.94	0.04
	Nagaland	6	-0.50	0.13
	Tripura	7	0.04	0.03

Now these estimated equations indicate that for any N.E State (i)

$$\frac{\delta NSDP_i}{\delta Fo_{ti}} = \hat{\beta}$$

$$\frac{\delta NSDP_i}{\delta FS_{ti}} = \hat{\gamma}_i$$

Thus (I = 1,2, ..7) represents the contribution of forests into the NSDP of the ith NE State. Similarly, (i=1,.2…7) representing the contribution of fishing in to the NSDP of the ith NE State.

Now we may compare with (where i and j represent two different N.E states).The difference between and may be subject to appropriate tests in order to ascertain if the difference between and (i.e -) were really statistically significant. The similar procedure may be adopted in order to examine the difference between and .

This study involves the use of t-tests in order to assess the significance of the difference between 's and between 's of 7 N.E. States. The t-difference matrices thus obtained have been presented through the Figure- 3 and 4 respectively.

4.7 t- difference Matrix

Figure 4.3: t-difference matrix of Forestry

	β_1	β_2	β_3	β_4	β_5	β_6	β_7
β_1	0	6.75*	0.67	0.79	6.81*	0.14	25.85*
β_2	-6.75*	0	-2.75*	-0.23	2.62*	-4.33*	6.25*
β_3	-0.67	2.75*	0	0.59	4.77*	-0.5	6.71*
β_4	-0.79	0.23	-0.59	0	1	-0.77	1.19
β_5	-6.81*	-2.62*	-4.77*	-1	0	-5.87*	0.57
β_6	-0.14	4.33*	0.5	0.77	5.87*	0	10.2*
β_7	-25.85*	-6.25*	-6.71*	-1.19	-0.57	-10.2*	0

Findings from the t-difference matrix (Forestry):

(i) Arunachal Pradesh gets greater contribution of forestry towards its NSDP than Assam, Mizoram and Tripura.

(ii) Assam's is greater than Mizoram and Tripura.

(iii) Mizoram gets greater contribution than Tripura

(iv) Tripura entails the lowest contribution of forestry in her NSDP among all the North-East states in our study.

(v) the t-difference is insignificant among Arunachal Pradesh, Meghalaya, Manipur, Meghalaya, and Nagaland. It implies that the contribution of forestry in the NSDP are almost the same in these states.

Figure 4.4: t-difference Matrix of Fishing

	γ_1	γ_2	γ_3	γ_4	γ_5	γ_6	γ_7
γ_1	0	-7.57*	-6.33*	-0.19	5.28*	-0.5	-10.16*
γ_2	7.57*	0	3*	2.33*	15*	3.53*	-1.6
γ_3	6.33*	-3*	0	1.6	18.75*	2.38*	-7.67*
γ_4	0.19	-2.33*	-1.62	0	1.95	-0.12	-2.71*
γ_5	-5.28*	-15*	-18.75*	-1.95	0	-3.38*	-19.6*
γ_6	0.5	-3.53*	-2.38*	0.12	3.38*	0	-4.15*
γ_7	10.16*	1.6	7.66*	2.71*	19.6*	4.15*	0

4.8 Findings:

from the t-difference matrix (Fishing):

(i) the t-difference between Assam and Tripura with respect to contribution of fishing towards NSDP is insignificant. It implies the contributions of fishing in NSDP in Assam and Tripura are almost equal.

(ii) Contribution of Fishing in the NSDP of Manipur, Meghalaya, Nagaland, Arunachal Pradesh and Mizoram are significantly (5% level) lower than Assam and Tripura.

(iii) Manipur entails a contribution which is greater than that for Meghalaya, Nagaland, Mizoram and Arunachal Pradesh

(iv) t-difference is insignificant (at even 10% level) in the case of Nagaland and Arunachal Pradesh.

(v) Mizoram ranks the lowest in the matter of getting contribution in NSDP from Fishing among all the North-East states.

4.9 Degree of Association

The last section of this study investigates the degree of association between the contribution of forestry and fishing among north-east states through rank correlation coefficient.

Table 4.4

States	*Rank in Forestry*	*Rank in Fishing*	*d*	*d^2*
Arunachal	1	4.5	-3.5	12.25
Assam	2	1	1	1
Manipur	1	2	-1	1

Meghalaya	1	3	-2	4
Mizoram	3	6	-3	9
Nagaland	1	4.5	-3.5	12.25
Tripura	4	1	3	9

Rank correlation coefficient is calculated by applying the formula R = 1- . In our study it is 0.13.

4.10 Summary and Conclusion

The value of R (rank correlation coefficient) implies that degree of association is negligible between forestry and fishing. Hence the contribution of Forestry to NSDP in any NE states is independent of that of Fishing to NSDP in that state.

REFERENCES:

Bhattacharjee R.P., *"Forest Resources in North Eastern region of India- a case study of Arunachal Pradesh in Forest Resources in North-East India."* Ed. B. Datta Ray and K. Alam (2002) Omsons Publications, New Delhi, pp. 268-269.

Bhattacharjee, R.P *"Forest Economy of Arunachal Pradesh" in Sustainable Management of Forests in India."* Ed. A Arunachal and M.L. Khan (2001). International Book distributors, Dehra Dun, pp. 517-525.

Hussain Zahid Ed (2003), *"Environmental Issues of North East India"*, Regency Publications

Mitra, A. and Chattopadhyay K., *Environment and Nature-Based Tourism An Endeavour at Sustainability*, Kaniska Publications, Foreworded by Professor C.K. Mukhopadhyay.

5

ARIMA Forecasting on Domestic Tourists' Arrival in Sikkim

5.1 Introduction

Sikkim is situated in the eastern Himalayas, with an area of 7096 sq km (constitutes 0.22% of the total geographical area of India) an altitude ranging from 800 to 28,208 ft and the climate ranging from tropical to alpine is one of the most beautiful states of the Indian Union. The state has diverse flora and fauna with rich culture, tradition, intricately designed handicrafts and handlooms, and honest and hospitable people. It is a landlocked state bounded on the north and north east by Tibet on the east by Bhutan, on the west by Nepal and on the South by the Darjeeling district of West Bengal. Sikkim has the potential to become the first 'poverty free' state in India by assuring every citizen social justice, equality and a decent standard of living. Sikkim is divided into four districts, north, south, east and west. The Gorkhaland agitation of Darjeeling hills in West Bengal makes Sikkim the paradise both for domestic as well as international tourists. The international tourists must obtain Inner Line Permit to visit Sikkim. This can be obtained from Delhi, Kolkata, Siliguri, Melli and Rangpo on the strength of an Indian Visa. The 15 days duration permit is issued on the spot on production of photocopies passport and visa details along with two passport size photos. The interested tourists for trekking in the interior regions of the state, the tourism department issued Protected Area Permits which is available for certain specified areas for groups of two or more foreigners. Anyway since the economy of the state depends heavily on tourism this paper tries to forecast the domestic tourist arrivals in Sikkim. The data are monthly type and is obtained from the tourism department, government of Sikkim.

5.2 Methodology

The publication of by Box and Jenkins of 'Time Series Analysis: Forecasting and Control' ushered in the new generation of forecasting tools. Popularly known as the Box-Jenkins methodology, but technically known as the ARIMA methodology, the emphasis of these methods is not on constructing single equation or simultaneous-equation models but on analyzing the probabilistic or stochastic properties of economic time series on their own under the philosophy of letting the data speak for themselves.

Generally the Box-Jenkins Approach Involves four Steps

(i) Identification

(ii) Estimation

(iii) Diagnostic checking and

(iv) Forecasting.

Step-1

Data must be stationary. If it is non-stationary it has to make stationary through differencing. Correlogram study that is time plot of ACFs (auto correlation functions) and PACFs (that is partial autocorrelation functions) can be used in this context. Generally the highest significant spike indicates the AR (Auto Regressive) process.

Step-2

After estimating the AR process we need to take the correlogram of the error series here the highest significant spike indicates the MA (Moving Average) process. Our ARIMA model now prepared. An ARMA (p,q) model in the variable differenced d times is equivalent to an ARIMA (p,d,q) model on the original data.

Step-3

Having chosen a particular ARIMA model, and having estimated its parameters we have to check whether the model fits the data well or not? Hence the diagnostic checking implies the residuals of the estimated ARIMA model should be white noise.

Step-4

The last step is forecasting. If at time t we want to forecast the outcome of y at time t+1, or yt+1. This is known as one- step ahead forecast .let ft denote the forecast of yt+1 made at time t, the forecast error is et= yt+1 -ft

5.3 Model Estimation: Further Elaboration

Let the ARIMA (p, d, q) model be

$$\theta(\beta)\Delta^d y_t = \varphi(\beta)\omega_t = \phi(\beta)\varepsilon_t \qquad \text{(i)}$$

With $\theta(\beta) = 1 - \varphi_1\beta - \varphi_2\beta^2 - - - - - \cdot\varphi_p\beta^p$

Equation (1) can be expressed in terms of error term series such that

$$\varepsilon_t = \varphi^{-1}(\beta)\theta(\beta)\omega_t \qquad \text{(ii)}$$

where $\omega_t = \Delta^d y_t$

The objective in estimation is to find a set of auto-regressive parameters (1, 2.... n) and a set of moving average parameters (1, 2, 3.... q) which minimize the sum of squared errors

$$S\{(\varphi_1,\varphi_2\ldots\varphi_n)\ (\theta_1,\theta_2,\theta_3\ldots\theta_q)\} = \sum\varepsilon_t^2 \qquad \text{(iii)}$$

Now let us assume that the error terms are all normally distributed and independent with mean 0 and variance . Then the conditional log-likelihood function associated with parameter values $\{(\varphi_1,\varphi_2\ldots\varphi_n)$ $(\theta_1,\theta_2,\theta_3\ldots\theta_q)\ ,\sigma\}$ is given by

$$L = -T\ \log\sigma^2 - S\{(\varphi_1,\varphi_2\ldots\varphi_n)\ (\theta_1,\theta_2,\theta_3\ldots\theta_q)\}/2\sigma^2 \qquad \text{(iv)}$$

Here L is the Conditional Logarithmic Likelihood function. Consequently,

$$\varepsilon_i = \omega_i - \varphi_1\omega_0 - \varphi_2\omega_{-1} \cdots\cdots\cdots\varphi_p\omega_{-p+1} + \theta_1\ldots\ldots\theta_4\varepsilon_{-q+1} \qquad \text{(v)}$$

Equation (iv) shows that the maximum-likelihood estimates of the model's parameters is given by the minimization of the sum of squared residuals. Thus under the assumption of normally distributed errors, the maximum-likelihood estimates is the same as least-square estimate.

But as far as tourist's arrival are concerned, there must be the seasonal impact on the data set, since December to April is the best time to visit Sikkim. Hence we need deseasonalize or seasonally adjusted data for forecasting.

5.4 Models of Seasonal Data

The ARIMA technique for modeling seasonal data is slightly different from that of nonseasonal data. The combination of strong seasonality and nonstationarity is often found in economic data. The ACF for a process with strong seasonality is similar to that for a non-seasonal process. The main difference is that the spikes a t lagss,2s,3s... do not exhibit rapid decay. If the autocorrelation at the seasonal lags do not decay, it is necessary to take the seasonal difference so that the other autocorrelations are not dwarfed by the seasonal effect. Thus we take the seasonal difference of the first difference. Two purely seasonal models for monthly data might be

$$X_t=\alpha_1 X_{t-12}+\xi_t \quad \text{(vi)}$$

and $X_t=\xi_t+\beta_1\xi_{t-12}$ (vii)

In practice, identification will be completed by the fact that the seasonal pattern will interact will interact with nonseasonal pattern in the data. The ACF and PACF for a combined seasonal/nonseasonal process will reflect both elements. Multiplicative seasonality allows for the interaction of the ARMA and the seasonal effects. Consider the multiplicative specifications,

$$(1-\alpha_1 L)X_t= (1+\beta_1 L)(1+\beta_{12}L_{12})\xi_t \quad \text{(viii)}$$

Many researchers prefer the multiplicative form since a rich interaction pattern can be captured with a small number of coefficients. Nevertheless, it is best to estimate several similar models and then select the best. For example,

$$m_t = \alpha_0 + \alpha_1 m_{t-1} + \xi_t + \beta_1 \xi_{t-1}$$

$$m_t = \alpha_0 + (1+\alpha_1 L)(1+\alpha_{12} L^{12}) m_{t-1} + \xi_t$$

$$m_t = \alpha_0 + (1+\beta_1 L)(1+\beta_{12} L_{12}) \xi_t$$

where is the seasonally adjusted stationary series. These are the three different types of model, AR (1) with seasonal MA, Multiplicative Autoregressive, and finally Multiplicative Moving average.

5.5 Empirical Findings

Figure 5.1: Time Plots of Domestic Tourists (Level) Arrival

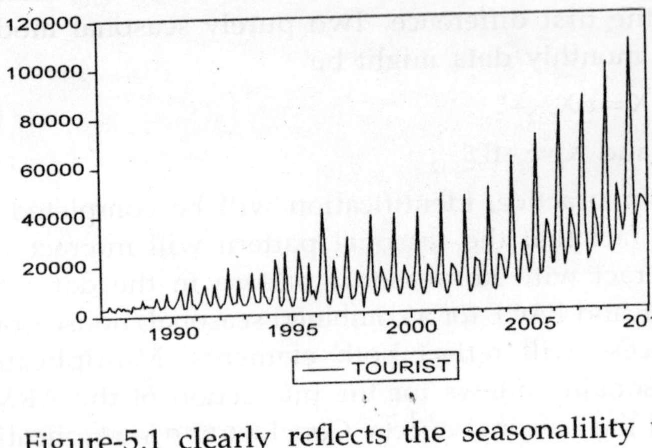

Figure-5.1 clearly reflects the seasonalility with trend in the data set. Therefore roughly we can say on the one hand there is non-stationarity and on the other hand seasonality pattern exists in the series. Hence to make it stationarity we need to do filtering of the data sets.

Figure 5.2: Time Plots of the Domestic Tourists (1st Difference) Arrival

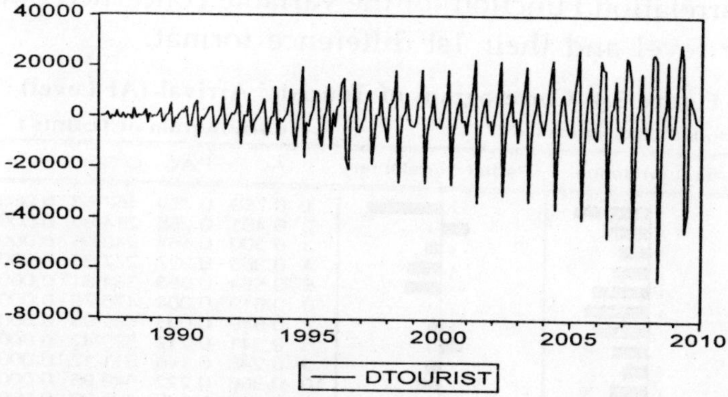

Figure-5.2 shows the time plot of tourists' arrival in their 1st difference stage. Which roughly shows a constant fluctuation among the mean value is disturbed by the seasonal impact. It suggests forecasting needs to neutralize the seasonal impact.

Figure 5.3: Time Plots of the Seasonally Adjusted Stationary Data Series of Tourists' Arrival

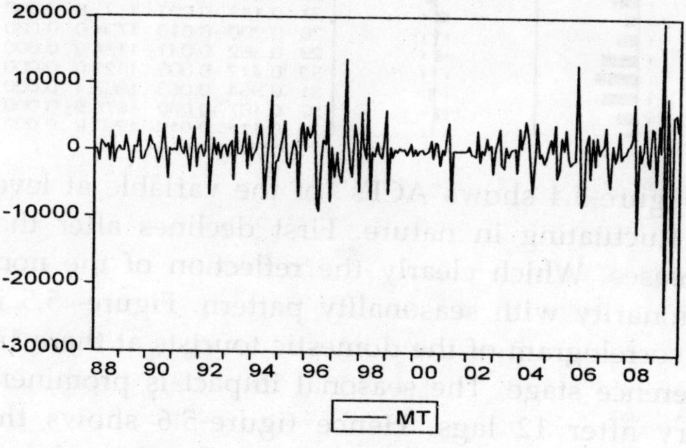

Figure 5.3 clearly shows the first two moments of the data set is invariant with time. For confirmation

of the seasonal pattern we need to explore the ACFs (Auto Correlation Function) and PACFs (Partial Auto Correlation Function) of the variable concerned both for level and their 1st difference format.

Figure 5.4: Correlogram of Tourists' Arrival (At Level)

Included observations: 277 Correlogram of TOURIST

Autocorrelation Partial Correlation

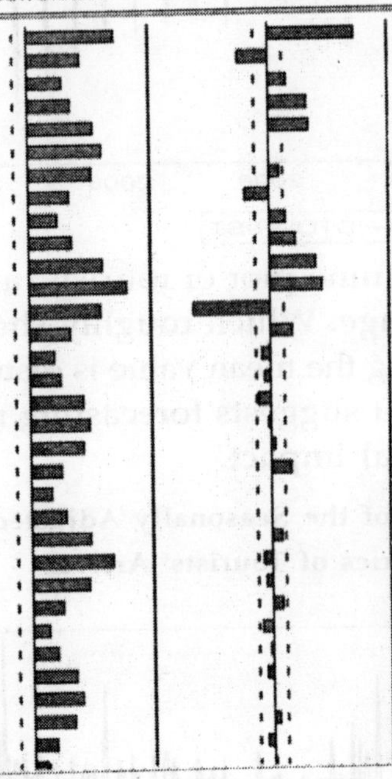

	AC	PAC	Q-Stat	Prob
1	0.750	0.750	157.53	0.000
2	0.451	-0.255	214.69	0.000
3	0.300	0.163	240.06	0.000
4	0.363	0.327	277.35	0.000
5	0.554	0.353	364.61	0.000
6	0.619	0.004	473.75	0.000
7	0.649	0.093	559.95	0.000
8	0.341	-0.212	593.42	0.000
9	0.248	0.146	611.12	0.000
10	0.366	0.222	649.95	0.000
11	0.618	0.406	760.88	0.000
12	0.832	0.443	962.94	0.000
13	0.612	-0.665	1072.4	0.000
14	0.342	0.181	1106.9	0.000
15	0.209	-0.070	1119.7	0.000
16	0.269	-0.044	1141.1	0.000
17	0.448	-0.113	1200.9	0.000
18	0.508	-0.024	1278.0	0.000
19	0.445	0.029	1337.4	0.000
20	0.262	0.172	1358.1	0.000
21	0.178	-0.004	1367.6	0.000
22	0.287	0.000	1392.6	0.000
23	0.513	0.084	1472.8	0.000
24	0.697	-0.080	1621.1	0.000
25	0.492	-0.056	1695.3	0.000
26	0.255	0.096	1715.3	0.000
27	0.143	-0.092	1721.6	0.000
28	0.200	-0.019	1734.0	0.000
29	0.362	-0.041	1774.9	0.000
30	0.412	-0.003	1828.0	0.000
31	0.364	0.053	1867.4	0.000
32	0.187	-0.042	1878.5	0.000
33	0.114	0.018	1882.6	0.000

Figure-5.4 shows ACFs of the variable at level are fluctuating in nature. First declines after that increases. Which clearly the reflection of the non-stationarity with seasonality pattern. Figure- 5.5 is the correlogram of the domestic tourists at there 1st difference stage. The seasonal impact is prominent every after 12 lags. Hence figure-5.6 shows the correlogram structure of the seasonally adjusted data sets.

Figure-5.5: Correlogram of Tourist Arrivals (At First Difference)

Included observations: 276

Correlogram of D(TOURIST)

Autocorrelation | Partial Correlation

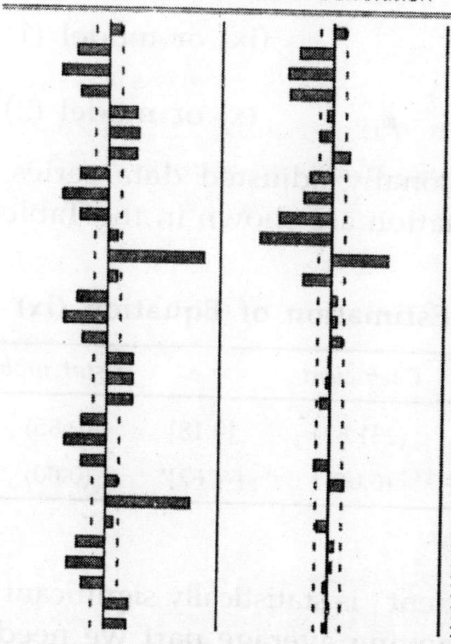

	AC	PAC	Q-Stat	Prob
1	0.099	0.099	2.7195	0.099
2	-0.302	-0.315	28.285	0.000
3	-0.437	-0.411	81.858	0.000
4	-0.259	-0.400	100.73	0.000
5	0.260	-0.043	119.92	0.000
6	0.278	-0.127	141.91	0.000
7	0.260	0.154	161.15	0.000
8	-0.256	-0.218	179.87	0.000
9	-0.420	-0.267	230.49	0.000
10	-0.256	-0.492	249.32	0.000
11	0.087	-0.663	251.50	0.000
12	0.889	0.523	481.05	0.000
13	0.096	-0.266	483.72	0.000
14	-0.280	0.042	506.75	0.000
15	-0.398	0.042	553.25	0.000
16	-0.231	0.099	568.96	0.000
17	0.246	-0.015	586.83	0.000
18	0.251	-0.026	605.53	0.000
19	0.238	-0.084	622.41	0.000
20	-0.237	-0,006	639.26	0.000
21	-0.381	-0.005	682.84	0.000
22	-0.225	-0.132	698.20	0.000
23	0.101	0.137	701.27	0.000
24	0.792	-0.005	892.03	0.000
25	0.060	-0.101	893.14	0.000
26	-0.257	0.052	913.34	0.000
27	-0.348	0.038	950.65	0.000
28	-0.203	-0.025	963.44	0.000
29	0.231	0.019	979.95	0.000
30	0.219	-0.026	994.97	0.000

Figure-5.6: Correlogram of the Tourist Arrivals (Seasonally Adjusted Data)

Sample: 1988:02 2010:01
Included observations: 264

Correlogram of MT

Autocorrelation | Partial Correlation

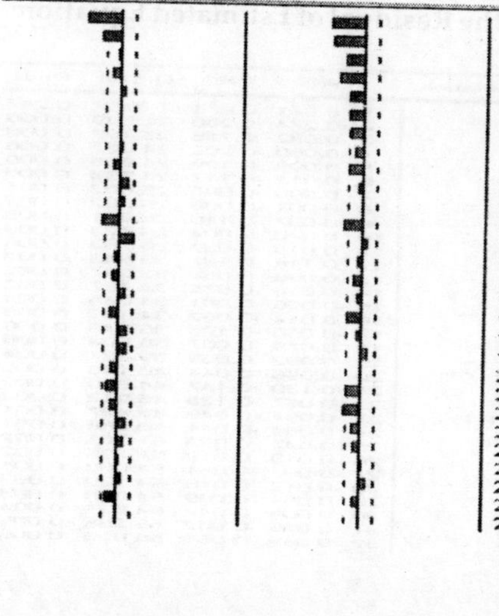

	AC	PAC	Q-Stat	Prob
1	-0.275	-0.276	20.166	0.000
2	-0.161	-0.256	27.122	0.000
3	-0.009	-0.157	27.144	0.000
4	-0.078	-0.207	28.771	0.000
5	0.027	-0.128	28.969	0.000
6	0.005	-0.118	28.977	0.000
7	-0.005	-0.103	28.985	0.000
8	0.018	-0.073	29.072	0.000
9	-0.053	-0.128	29.842	0.000
10	0.066	-0.027	31.064	0.001
11	0.031	0.004	31.323	0.001
12	-0.139	-0.153	36.741	0.000
13	0.127	0.028	41.264	0.000
14	-0.033	-0.039	41.579	0.000
15	-0.051	-0.071	42.324	0.000
16	0.047	-0.032	42.939	0.000
17	-0.079	-0.125	44.725	0.000
18	0.069	-0.035	46.078	0.000
19	0.073	0.042	47.611	0.000
20	-0.047	0.000	48.247	0.000
21	-0.085	-0.118	50.354	0.000
22	-0.048	-0.142	51.018	0.000
23	0.082	-0.063	52.955	0.000
24	0.047	-0.066	53.596	0.000
25	0.019	0.020	53.704	0.001
26	0.034	0.045	54.050	0.001
27	-0.093	-0.044	56.621	0.001
28	0.004	0.006	56.625	0.001

From figure-5 it is clear that lag 1 and 2 are significant. Therefore the possible model with AR structures one and two are

$$m_t = \alpha + \beta m_{t-1} + \mu_t \qquad \text{(ix) or model (1)}$$

$$m_t = \alpha + \beta m_{t-1} + \beta_1 m_{t-2} + \mu_t \qquad \text{(x) or model (2)}$$

where, is the seasonally adjusted data series. The results of the estimation are shown in the Table below.

Table 5.1: Results of Estimation of Equation (ix)

Parameter	*Coefficient*	*s.e*	*t-stat prob*
α = 41.72	(231.63)	[0.18]	(0.85)
β = -0.28	(0.06)	[-4.62]*	(0.00)

R^2 = 0.08, adjusted R^2 = 0.07

The estimated coefficient is statistically significant. Now to find out the moving average part we need to take the correlogram of the error series. Figure-7 shows this. From this figure it is clear that lag 2 is significant.

Figure 5.7: Correlogram of the Residual of Estimated Equation

Included observations: 263

Autocorrelation | Partial Correlation

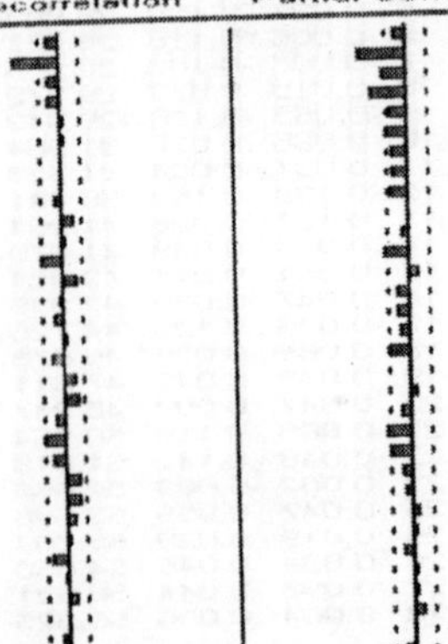

	AC	PAC	Q-Stat	Prob
1	-0.071	-0.071	1.3407	0.247
2	-0.274	-0.280	21.389	0.000
3	-0.082	-0.138	23.189	0.000
4	-0.080	-0.202	24.932	0.000
5	0.009	-0.106	24.955	0.000
6	0.012	-0.117	24.995	0.000
7	0.005	-0.085	25.002	0.001
8	-0.001	-0.086	25.002	0.002
9	-0.037	-0.110	25.371	0.003
10	0.070	0.004	26.723	0.003
11	0.015	-0.037	26.783	0.005
12	-0.116	-0.137	30.643	0.002
13	0.096	0.053	33.097	0.002
14	-0.016	-0.075	33.167	0.003
15	-0.056	-0.061	34.045	0.003
16	0.014	-0.052	34.102	0.005
17	-0.058	-0.125	35.046	0.006
18	0.079	0.007	36.804	0.006
19	0.092	0.038	39.227	0.004
20	-0.056	-0.044	40.125	0.005
21	-0.130	-0.147	44.960	0.002
22	-0.057	-0.123	45.912	0.002
23	0.094	-0.049	48.497	0.001
24	0.084	-0.041	50.568	0.001
25	0.047	0.039	51.201	0.002
26	0.018	0.019	51.296	0.002
27	-0.097	-0.051	54.080	0.001
28	-0.012	0.018	54.120	0.002
29	0.051	0.009	54.888	0.003
30	0.006	0.042	54.897	0.004
31	-0.036	-0.002	55.285	0.006
32	-0.049	-0.063	56.020	0.005

Therefore our ARIMA structure (seasonally adjusted) becomes

$$m_t = \alpha + \beta m_{t-1} + \beta_1 \mu_{t-2} + \xi_t \qquad \text{(xi)}$$

The estimation of equation (xi) is shown below.

Table 5.2: Results of Estimation of Equation (xi)

Parameter	*Coefficient*	*s.e*	*t-stat*	*prob*
α	36.21	(223.39)	[0.16]	(0.87)
	-0.37	(0.06)	[-6.22]*	(0.00)
	-0.32	(0.06)	[-4.95]*	(0.00)

R-² 0.15   Adj R^2 = 0.14

Figure 5.8: Correlogram of the Error Series of Estimated (xi)

Included observations: 261

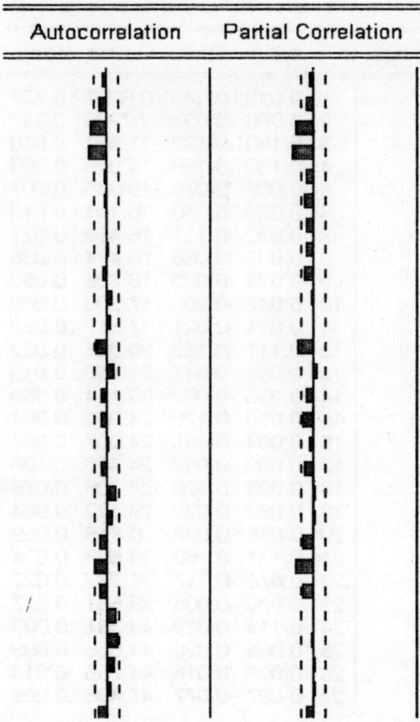

Lag	AC	PAC	Q-Stat	Prob
1	-0.034	-0.034	0.3023	0.582
2	-0.064	-0.065	1.3800	0.502
3	-0.162	-0.167	8.3250	0.040
4	-0.178	-0.202	16.790	0.002
5	-0.017	-0.068	16.865	0.005
6	-0.012	-0.082	16.904	0.010
7	0.008	-0.079	16.922	0.018
8	0.011	-0.062	16.956	0.031
9	-0.038	-0.091	17.341	0.044
10	0.041	-0.011	17.801	0.058
11	0.030	-0.006	18.046	0.081
12	-0.108	-0.151	21.254	0.047
13	0.080	0.041	23.011	0.042
14	-0.047	-0.063	23.622	0.051
15	-0.057	-0.113	24.525	0.057
16	0.018	-0.041	24.615	0.077
17	-0.046	-0.088	25.217	0.090
18	0.090	0.013	27.488	0.070
19	0.056	0.014	28.383	0.076
20	-0.060	-0.099	29.393	0.080
21	-0.115	-0.173	33.200	0.044
22	-0.070	-0.104	34.617	0.042
23	0.089	0.007	36.922	0.033
24	0.108	-0.009	40.280	0.020
25	0.071	0.019	41.727	0.019
26	0.038	0.011	42.152	0.024
27	-0.085	-0.063	44.282	0.019

of ACFs and PACFs are significant. Other lags are not significant. Therefore the residuals are not purely random but more or less random. Now considering second model,

Table 5.3: Results of Estimation of Equation (x)

Parameter	*Coefficient*	*s.e*	*t-stat*	*prob*
α	43.65	(224.9)	[0.19]	0.84
	-0.34	(0.06)	[-5.79]*	0.00
	-0.26	(0.06)	[-4.32]*	0.00

R-squared = 0.137

Adjusted R-squared = 0.131

Figure 5.9: Correlogram of the Error Series of Estimated (x)

Included observations: 261

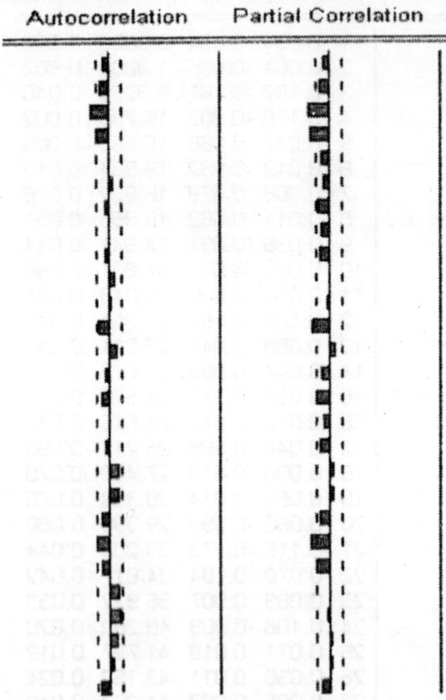

	AC	PAC	Q-Stat	Prob
1	-0.049	-0.049	0.6297	0.427
2	-0.090	-0.093	2.7980	0.247
3	-0.180	-0.192	11.431	0.010
4	-0.130	-0.169	15.928	0.003
5	-0.008	-0.076	15.945	0.007
6	0.030	-0.050	16.191	0.013
7	-0.032	-0.111	16.468	0.021
8	0.005	-0.058	16.474	0.036
9	-0.034	-0.082	16.798	0.052
10	0.047	-0.006	17.395	0.066
11	0.021	-0.021	17.517	0.093
12	-0.111	-0.153	20.905	0.052
13	0.082	0.047	22.758	0.045
14	-0.036	-0.062	23.124	0.058
15	-0.059	-0.120	24.091	0.064
16	0.004	-0.055	24.097	0.087
17	-0.038	-0.092	24.499	0.106
18	0.098	0.028	27.206	0.075
19	0.082	0.029	29.122	0.064
20	-0.075	-0.098	30.715	0.059
21	-0.131	-0.169	35.599	0.024
22	-0.075	-0.117	37.232	0.022
23	0.090	-0.006	39.581	0.017
24	0.114	-0.019	43.331	0.009
25	0.065	0.020	44.566	0.009
26	0.025	0.016	44.755	0.013
27	-0.097	-0.077	47.498	0.009

complete ARIMA model (2) is

$$m_t = \alpha + \beta m_{t-1} + \beta_1 m_{t-2} + \beta_2 \mu_{t,-3} + \xi_t \quad \text{(xii)}$$

Table 5.4: Results of the Estimation of Equation(xii)

Parameter	*Coefficient*	*s.e*	*t-stat*	*prob*
α	39.45027	221.2020	0.178345	0.8586
	-0.432611	0.062570	-6.9140*	0.0000
	-0.378514	0.066106	-5.7258*	0.0000
	-0.277099	0.069860	-3.9664*	0.0001

R^2=0.187 Adj R^2 = 0.178

Figure 5.9: Correlogram of the Residual of Complete Model(2)

Included observations: 259

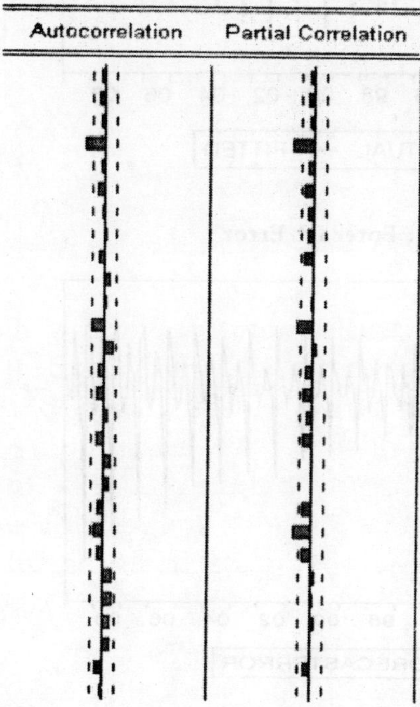

	AC	PAC	Q-Stat	Prob
1	-0.028	-0.028	0.2088	0.648
2	-0.045	-0.046	0.7415	0.690
3	-0.031	-0.034	1.0003	0.801
4	-0.194	-0.199	11.020	0.026
5	-0.035	-0.054	11.353	0.045
6	-0.068	-0.098	12.602	0.050
7	-0.020	-0.050	12.708	0.080
8	0.014	-0.046	12.763	0.120
9	-0.048	-0.086	13.394	0.146
10	0.044	-0.006	13.927	0.176
11	0.023	-0.010	14.065	0.229
12	-0.127	-0.157	18.463	0.102
13	0.082	0.037	20.332	0.087
14	-0.055	-0.079	21.152	0.098
15	-0.060	-0.090	22.156	0.104
16	0.034	-0.041	22.469	0.129
17	-0.065	-0.088	23.631	0.130
18	0.066	-0.002	24.856	0.129
19	0.043	-0.003	25.386	0.148
20	-0.057	-0.095	26.295	0.156
21	-0.087	-0.170	28.427	0.128
22	-0.051	-0.090	29.183	0.140
23	0.089	0.029	31.440	0.112
24	0.087	0.009	33.636	0.091
25	0.068	0.035	34.981	0.089
26	0.063	0.006	36.121	0.089
27	-0.066	-0.069	37.373	0.088
28	-0.015	0.003	37.437	0.110

Figure 5.9 shows only one significant spike. Hence model (2) can be treated as a better model for forecasting compared to model (1). Now on the basis of model (2) we forecast and calculate the forecast error.

Figure 5.10: Actual Value and ARIMA fitted Value

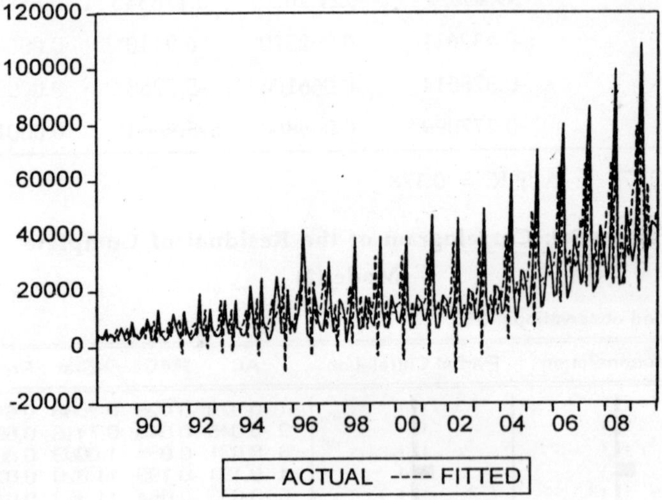

Figure 5.11: Forecast Error

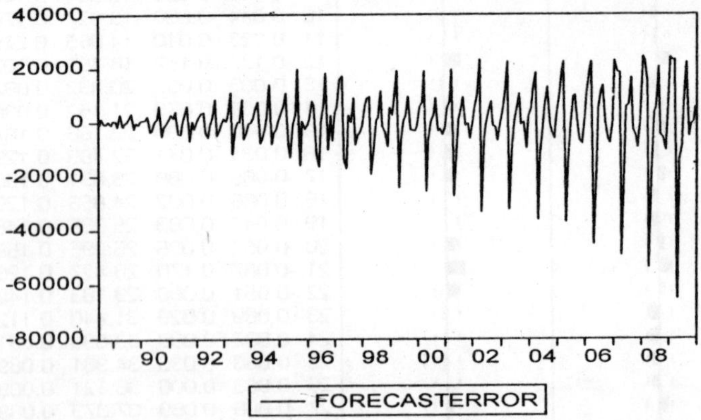

Table 5.5: Actual Value and Forecasted Value (Out of Sample)

Year	*Actual value*	*Forecasted value*
2010:01	40160	40002
2010:02		48902
2010:03		65181
2010:04		88696
2010:05		110756

Figure 5.12: Forecasting (Out of Sample Period)

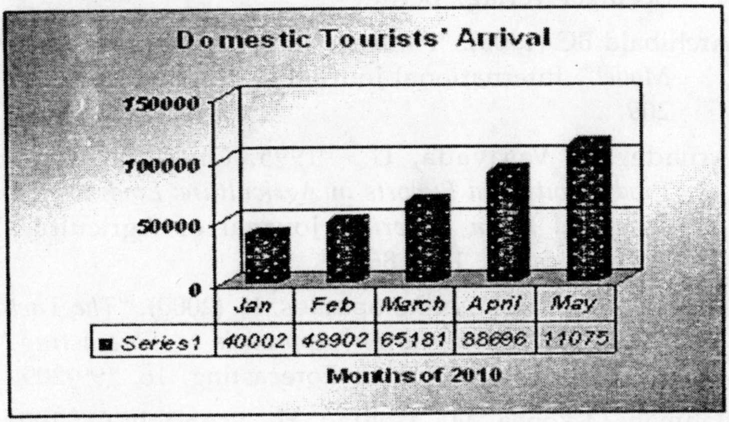

5.6 Conclusion

From the Table-5.5 and Figure 5.12 it is clear that according to our fitted model in May 2010 the domestic tourists' in Sikkim should cross five digits number. So the government of Sikkim should be careful so that the environment of Chhangu, Baba Mandir , Yumthang ,snowfalls of Lachung Bazar can not be disturbed.

REFERENCES

Akaike, H., 1969. *Fitting Autoregressive Models for Prediction*. Annals of the Institute of Statistical Mathematics 21, 243-247.

Anderson BDO, Moore JB (1979). *Optimal Filtering*. Prentice-Hall, Englewood Cliffs.

Ansely, C. F. (1979). *An algorithm for the exact likelihood of a mixed autoregressive-moving average process*, Biometrika 66: 59{65.

Aoki M (1987). *State Space Modeling of Time Series*. Springer-Verlag, Berlin.

Archibald BC (1900). "*Parameter Space of the Holt-Winters Model*". International Journal of Forecasting, 6, 199-209.

Arnade, C., Vasavada, U., 1995. *Causality between Productivity and Exports in Agriculture: Evidence from Asia and Latin America*. Journal of Agricultural Economics 46, 174-186.

Assimakopoulos, V., Nikolopoulos, K. (2000). "*The Theta Model: a Decomposition Approach to Forecasting.*" International Journal of Forecasting, 16, 199-209.

Bahmani-Oskooee, M., Mohtad, H., Shabsigh, G., 1991. "*Export, Growth and Causality in LDCs: a RE-examination*". Journal of Development Economics 36, 405-415.

Blalock, G., Gertler, P.J., 2004. "*Learning from Exporting Revisited in A Less Developed Setting*". Journal of Development Economics 75 , 397-416.

Boero, G. and Marrocu, E.: "*2002, The Performance of Non-linear Exchange Rate Models: A Forecasting Comparison*", Journal of Forecasting 21, 512-3-542.

Bowerman, BL, O'Connel, R.T., Koehler, A.B. (2005). *Forecasting Time series and Regression: An Applied Approach*. Thomson Brooks/ Cole, Belmont CA.

Box, George, and Gwilym Jenkins. *Time Series Analysis, Forecasting, and Control*. San Francisco: Holden Day, 1976.

Box, G.E.P. and Jenkins, G.M.: 1970, *Time Series Analysis, Forecasting and Control*, Holden-Day, San Francisco.

Brailsford, T.J. and Faff, R.W. (1996): *"An Evaluation of Volatility Forecasting Techniques"*, Journal of Banking and Finance, 20, 419-438.

Brannas, K., and De Gooijer, J.G.: 1994, *"Autoregressive-Asymmetric Moving Average Model for Business Cycle Data"*, Journal of Forecasting 13, 529-544.

Brockwell, P.J., Davis, R.A. (1991). *Time Series: Theory and Methods*. Springer-Verlag, New York, 2nd edition.

Chatfield, C., Yar, M. (1991), *"Prediction Intervals for Multiplicatives Holt-Winters"* International Journal of Forecasting, 7, 31-37.

Choi, I, 1993. *"Asymptotic Normality of the Least Squares Estimates for Higher order Autoregressive Integrated Process with Some Applications"*. Econometric Theory 9,263-282.

Clements, M.P., Franses, P.H. and Swanson. N.R.: 2004, *Forecasting Economic and Financial Time Series with Non–Linear Models*, International Journal of Forecasting 20,169-183

Deutsch, M, Granger, C.W.J. and Terasvirta, T.: 1994, *"The Combination of Forecasts Using Changing Weights"* International Journal of Forecasting 10, 47-57.

Enders, Walter. (*ARIMA and Cointegration Tests of Purchasing Power Parity.*" Review of Economics and Statistics 70(Aug.1988), 504-08

Engle, R.F. (1982). *Autoregressive conditional heteroscedasticity*, with estimates of the variance of United Kingdoms inflations, Econometrica 50: 987-1007.

Garner Jr E.S. McKenzie, E. (1985). *"Forecasting Trends in Time Series."* Management Science, 31 (100, 1237-1246).

Granger, CW.J. and Pesaran,M.H., 2000, *"Economic and Statistical Measures of Forecast Accuracy"*, Journal of Forecasting 19, 537-560.

Granger, C. and Newbold, P. (1986). *Forecasting Economic Time Series*, 2nd edn, San Diego: Academic Press.

Hannan, E. J. and Rissanen, J. (1982). *Recursive estimation of mixed atoregressive-moving average order*, Biometrika 69: 81-94.

Ljung, G. M. and Box, G. E. P. (1978). *On a measure of lack of □t in time-series models*, Biometrika 65: 297-303.

LÄutkepohl, H. (2004). *Univariate time series analysis, in H. LÄutkepohl and M. KrÄatzig (eds), Applied Time Series Econometrics*, Cambridge University Press, Cambridge, pp. 8-85.

Mukhopadhyay C.K and Kundu Amit, (March 2008), *"Arima Forecasting for Exchange Rate (INR/NR) Quoted in Indo-Nepal Trade: A Study with Box-Jenkins Methodology"* Journal of Regional Economic Studies, Department of Economics, University of North Bengal, page 50-70

Pindyck, R.S., D.L. Rubinfeld (2001) *Econometric Models and Economic Forecasts (4th edition)*,Irwin- McGraw-Hill, New York.

West, K.D., 2006, *"Forecast Evaluation"* in G. Elliott, CW.J Granger and A. Timmermann (eds.), Handbook of Economic Forecasting, Elsevier, Amsterdam.

6

Rice Production in Assam—A Brief Note

Rice is grown in many regions across India. For about 65% of the people living in India, rice is a staple food for them. Rice is essential to life in India. It is a part of nearly every meal, and it is grown on a majority of the rural farms. It is one of the important cereal food crops of India. Rice contributes about 43% of total food grain production and 46% of total cereal production in the country. It continues to play vital role in the national exports. Rice export contributes nearly 25% of total agriculture export from the country.

Agriculture is the main source of income for families in India. Farms cover over half the land and almost three-quarters of that land is used to grow the two major grains: rice and wheat. India is the second leading producer of rice in the entire world, preceded only by China. India's annual rice production is around 85-90 million tons. Food Corporation of India purchases around 20 to 25% of the total rice production in the country both under levy from the rice mills and directly in the form of paddy from the farmers.

More than 4000 varieties of rice are grown in India.

India is the world's largest exporter of Basmati rice to Saudi Arabia and other Middle East Countries, Europe, and the United States.

India has the potential to export one million tons of Basmati rice.

Major destinations for Indian non-basmati, white/ parboiled rice are Bangladesh, Indonesia, Philippines, Nigeria, South Africa, Ivory Coast, and other African countries.

Worldwide, there are more than 40,000 different varieties of rice. Often times, rice is categorized by its size as being either short grain, medium grain or long grain. Short grain, which has the highest starch content, makes the stickiest rice, while long grain is lighter and tends to remain separate when cooked. The qualities of medium grain fall between the other two types. Another way that rice is classified is according to the degree of milling that it undergoes. This is what makes a brown rice different than white rice. Thus, the primary differences in different varieties of rice are their cooking characteristics, shapes and even colors and in some cases, a subtle flavor difference. The influx of convenience foods has brought consumers rice in bags, packets and cartons. Rice can be purchased cooked or uncooked, packed, dehydrated and also frozen. To meet the many special requirements of packaged foods, rice undergoes varying degrees of processing, including regular-milled, parboiled, precooked, and brown.

Worldwide, India stands first in rice area and second in rice production, after China. It contributes 21.5 percent of global rice production. Within the country, rice occupies one-quarter of the total cropped area, contributes about 40 to 43 percent of total food grain production and continues to play a vital role in the national food and livelihood security system. However, India did not become a major rice exporting country for a long time. Its share in world rice trade, mainly in the form of small-volume exports of highly prized basmati rice, was insignificant (5 percent). It was not until the mid-1980s that the quantum of export started to grow, from 110 000 tonnes in 1978/79 to 890 613 tonnes in 1994/95 and to a record 5.5 million tonnes in 1995/96, second only to Thailand (at 5.9 million tonnes).Among the exporting countries, Thailand, Vietnam, India and Pakistan are the major countries exporting rice in sizeable quantity. West Bengal, Uttar Pradesh, Andhra Pradesh, Punjab, Tamil Nadu, Bihar, Orissa, Assam, Karnataka and Haryana are the major producing states.

The economy of Assam is predominantly agrarian. About 99 per cent area of total land mass of the State is rural and almost 50 per cent of the total land area is used for cultivation. The net cultivated area of the State is 27.53 lakh hectares (2004-05) of which 23 per cent area is either flood or draught prone and the per capita availability of net sown area comes to around 0.1 hectare. The average operational holding is 1.15 hectare only and more than 83 per cent of the farmer family is small and marginal farmers. The contribution of the agriculture sector to the GSDP (at constant prices; 1999-2000 prices) was pegged at 22.85 per cent in 2007-08(Quick estimate) after steady decline from 32.24 per cent in 1999-2000. However, this sector continues to support more than 75 per cent population of the State directly or indirectly providing employment of more than 53 per cent of the workforce.

The soil, topography, rainfall and climate of the State in general are congenial for agricultural activities mainly for cultivation of paddy crops. Paddy cultivation occupies 86.56 per cent of the net cropped area and 61.16 per cent of the Gross Cropped area. The normal paddy area of the State is 23.83 Lakh hectares.

Rice is main crop of Assam and three crops are grown in a year i.e. Autumn, Winter and Summer crops. In Assam state rice productivity is medium-low to very low, therefore, average yield of rice is very poor. It is grown in 23 districts of the state. Out of this 11 districts are coming under medium low productivity i.e., yield ranging between 1,500-2,000 kg/ha. Average area under rice in medium-low productivity group comprising of 11 districts during triennium ending 2000-2001 was 10.20 lakh hectares, which was 39.5% of average area under rice i.e., 25.82 lakh hectares in the state during the same period. Average production of rice during the same triennium was 17.92 lakh tonnes, which was 48.4% of average production of rice in the state. Average productivity of rice in medium-low productivity group comprising of 11 districts during triennium ending 2000-2001 was 1,757 kg/ha, which was more than the state's average productivity of 1,435 kg/ha but less than the national average productivity of 1,947 kg/ha during the same period.

Another 11 districts are falling under low productivity group i.e., yield ranging between 1,000-

1,500 kg/ha. Average area under rice in low productivity group during triennium ending 2000-2001 was 14.63 lakh hectares, which was 56.7% of average area under rice in the state. Average production of rice in low productivity group comprising of 11 districts during triennium ending 2000-2001 was 18.15 lakh tonnes, which was 49.0% of triennium average of total production of rice in the state.

Triennium average productivity of rice in low productivity group comprising of 11 districts was 1,240 kg/ha, which was less than the state's triennium average productivity of 1,435 kg/ha.

One district is coming under very low productivity i.e., yield below 1,000 kg/ha. Average area under rice in this district during triennium ending 2000-2001 was 0.99 lakh hectares, which was 3.8% of total average rice area in the state during the same period. Triennium average production in this district was 0.98 lakh tonnes, which was 2.6% of triennium average production of rice in the State. Triennium average productivity of rice in low productivity district was 990 kg/ha, which was very much less than the average productivity of the State.

Productivity of rice in Assam is very poor, more than 50% rice cultivation in Assam is concentrated in low productivity zone and about 40% rice is cultivated in medium-low productivity zone. Thus, rice productivity of Assam is much below the average productivity of the nation. Irrigation facility is very much less in Assam, only 22% irrigation facility is available in Assam for rice crop. Besides, rice area coverage under high yielding variety is below 45%.

Area, production and productivity of rice under different productivity groups in Assam during triennium ending 2000-2001 are given in table below.

Productivity groups	*No. of Districts*	*Area (mil.Ha) Rice*	*% of State's Rice Area*	*Production in Lakh Tonnes*	*% of State's Rice Production*	*Productivity (Kg/Ha.)*
High Productivity (> 2,500 Kg/Ha)	-	-	-	-	-	-
Medium Productivity (> 2,000-2,500 Kg/Ha)	-	-	-	-	-	-
Medium-Low Productivity (> 1,500-2,000 Kg/Ha)	11	10.20	39.5	17.92	48.4	1757
Low Productivity (1,000-1,500 Kg/Ha)	11	14.63	56.7	18.15	49	1240
Very-Low Productivity (< 1,000 Kg/Ha)	1	00.99	03.8	00.98	02.6	990
TOTAL	23	25.82	100	37.5		1435

Based on geohydrological and physiographic characteristics, the state is divided into six broad Agroclimatic zones, namely,

North Bank Plains Zone (NBPZ): This zone comprising the district of Dhemaji, North Lakhimpur, Sonitpur and Darrang, stretches over an area of is14, 424-sq. km. which accounts for 18.37 per cent of the state area.

Upper Brahmaputra Valley Zone (UBVZ): It includes the district of Sibsagar, Jorhat, Tinsukia, Dibrugarh and Golaghat with an area of 16078.9-sq. km., which is 21 per cent of the state area.

Central Brahmaputra Valley Zone (CBVZ): Comprises the district of Nagaon and Marigaon with an area of 5561-sq. km., which is 7.08 per cent of the state area.

Lower Brahmaputra Valley Zone (LBVZ): Comprises of the district of Kamrup, Barpeta, Nalbari, Dhubri, Goalpara and Bangaigaon with an area 20,222-sq. km., which accounts for 25.75 per cent of the state area.

Barak Valley Zone (BVZ): It covers about 8.84 per cent (6941.2-sq.km.) of the state's total geographical area and comprises the district of Cachar, Karimganj and Hailakandi.

Hills Zones (HZ): Comprises the district of Karbi Anglong and North Cachar Hills with an area of 15,222-sq. km., which is a19.40 per cent of the state area.

There is distinct variation in climate, cropping pattern, cropping intensity, production and productivity in different agroclimatic zones due to difference in physioraphy, rainfall, temperature and soils.

Kalita and Baruah (1992) using coefficient of variation in Assam examined the degree of instability in different types of rice. They found that the highest and considerable instability in productivity was associated with summer rice. Winter rice was found to be the most stable crop in the case of productivity. However , the growth in productivity of different type of rice was found to be very low or negligible due to slow development of irrigation facilities, gradual degradation of the nutrient status of the soil in the state and increasing damage of standing crop by natural hazards. Development of effective irrigation facilities with proper technology and planning are the prime needs for increasing the rice productivity in the state, are some of the recommendations given by the researchers.

Bhowmick and Ahmed (1993) worked out the growth of area, production and productivity of oilseeds in Assam by fitting linear and exponential function and concluded that the increase in production was mainly due to increase in acreage only. Productivity was noted to be more or less stagnant which could be attributed to poor adoption of improved technology. Acreage under oilseed crops was found to be influenced by lagged area, lagged yield, lagged relative yield and to some extent yield risk and lagged farm harvest price. They laid emphasis on vigorous extension work for spreading improved technology for oilseeds production among the farmers.

Summer rice is known by different names in different parts of our country. For example: it is also known as known as 'Boro' in Assam and West Bengal, 'Dalua' in Orissa, 'Dalwa' in Andhra Pradesh, 'Punja' in Kerala and 'Navarai' in Tamil Nadu and 'Garma' in Bihar.

The production of Rice in the State, as per final estimates, during the year 2007-08 was 33.19 lakh MT as against 29.16 lakh MT in 2006-07 showing an increase of 13.8 per cent over the previous year. However, production of rice was 6.56 per cent low during the year compared to the rice production during 2005-06. Due to satisfactory departmental efforts, the production of pulses during the year 2007-08 was estimated at 0.63 lakh MT with an increase of 6.78 per cent as against 0.59 lakh MT during 2006-07.

During the year 2005-06 the production of pulses was 0.56 lakh MT. An impressive increase in production of oilseeds with 1.35 lakh MT was witnessed during the year 2007-08 as against 1.29 lakh MT in 2006-07. The production of oilseeds during 2005-06 was 1.10 lakh.Poor connectivity is a hindrance to higher growth but higher outlays indicate the State's keenness to correct it. Infrastructure development therefore remains high on the agenda of policy intervention. To improve the reach of the National Highways in the NER, 4-laning of 678 km length has been taken up as part of East-West Corridor and 1,246 km length identified for 4-laning under NHDP-III on BOT basis. The SARDP-NE) has also been rolled out. Assam accounts for 50% of India's domestic onshore oil production, has four out of its twelve refineries with a refining capacity of 7 million tones and the biggest pool of oil & gas professionals. The Government of India continues to offer exploration blocks and discovered fields to various private/ joint venture parties as well.

Yield Rate(Kg./Hect.) of Principal Agricultural Crops in Assam:

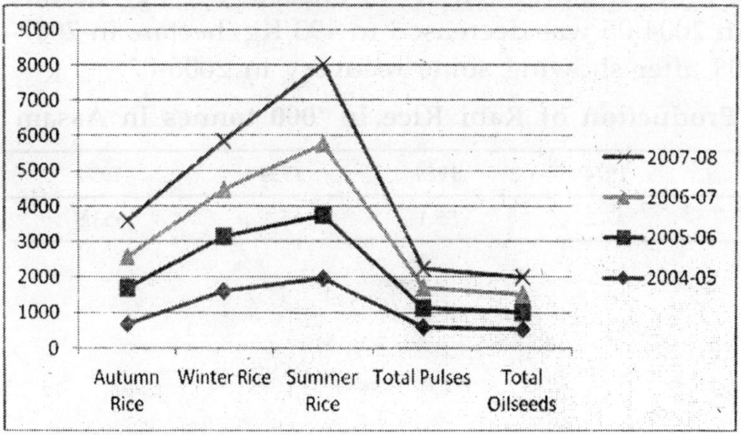

Source: Economic Survey Assam 2008-09

The trend of yield rate of Autumn Rice is fluctuating. During 2005-06 the yield rate was increased to 1016 Kg/ hectare from 667 Kg./ hectare in 2004-05, again it is decreased to 899 Kg/hectare during 2006-07. The yield rate of the Autumn Rice was 999 Kg/hectare during 2007-08. The yield rate of Winter Rice maintains its decreasing trend during the years from 2004-05 to 2007-08. However, the yield rate (Kg./ hectare) of Winter paddy was marginally high during 2007-08 compared to the yield rate in 2006-07. The yield rate of Winter rice was low during the years 2006-07 and 2007-08 over the previous two years. It was because the State had experienced drought like situation and severe floods during the peak Sali Paddy seasons during the years 2006-07 and 2007-08 respectively. The productivity of Summer Paddy, on the other hand, maintains its increasing trend during the period 2004-05 to 2007-08 except in the year 2005-06. The trend of productivity of pulses was erratic during the period.

The trend of productivity of Oil Seeds was also erratic. The productivity of oilseeds 535 kg/ hectare in 2004-05 was decreased to 493 Kg/hectare in 2007-08 after showing some recovery in 2006-07.

Production of Rabi Rice in '000 tonnes in Assam

1974	*1984*	*1994*	*1994*
47.2	55.1	55.1	653.8

Area, Production and Average Yield of Some Important Crops in Assam:

(Area in thousand hectares, Production in thousand tones and Average yield inn Kg/hectare)

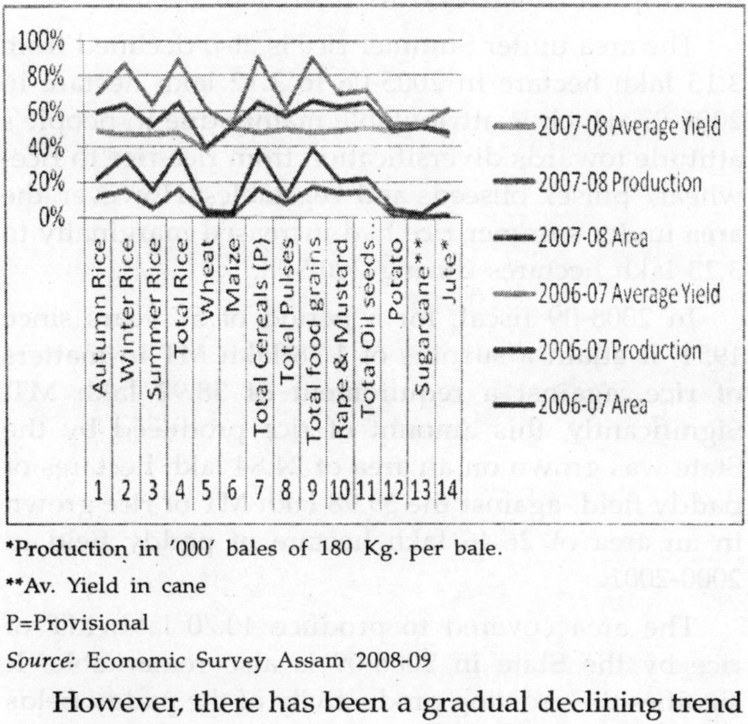

*Production in '000' bales of 180 Kg. per bale.

**Av. Yield in cane

P=Provisional

Source: Economic Survey Assam 2008-09

However, there has been a gradual declining trend in area under Autumn Rice, which has switched over to the Summer Rice due to its higher productivity and hazard risk. During 2005-06, the area under Autumn Rice was 3.98 lakh hectares, further declined to 3.79 lakh hectare during 2006-07. Final forecast estimates shows that the area under autumn rice had further declined to 3.54 lakh hectares during 2007-08.

The area under Winter rice, the principal Kharif Crop which registered a major set back during the year 2006-07 and enabled to cover only 14.98 lakh hectares as against 17.07 lakh hectares during the year 2005-06 as the State suffered a serious drought like situation. During 2007-08, the area coverage under the crop had increased to 16.47 lakh hectares.

The area under Summer rice is also declined from 3.15 lakh hectare in 2005-06 to 3.12 lakh hectare in 2006-07 which is attributable mainly due to people's attitude towards diversification from rice-rice to rice-wheat/ pulse/ oilseeds and vegetables. However, the area under summer rice had increased marginally to 3.23 lakh hectares during 2007-08.

In 2008-09 fiscal, for a period of 57 years since 1951, it attain a surplus of 1.78 lakh MT in matters of rice, against a requirement of 38.92 lakh MT. Significantly, this amount of rice produced by the State was grown on an area of 24.84 lakh hectares of paddy field, against the 39.98 lakh MT of rice grown in an area of 26.46 lakh hectare of paddy field in 2000-2001.

The area covered to produce 40.70 lakh MT of rice by the State in 2008-09 is also remarkable. It signifies the growing productivity of the paddy fields for various reasons. The State could produce 5.58 lakh MT of autumn rice on an area of 5.40 lakh hectare in 2000-2001. The same year, it could produce 27.60 Lakh MT of winter rice on an area of 17.77 lakh hectare, while the area required by it during that year to produce 6.80 lakh MT of summer rice, was 3.29 lakh hectare.

From the point of productivity also, summer rice is more productive. The normal productivity of autumn rice in the State is 896 kg per hectare, while it is

1,482 kg per hectare in the case of winter rice. But, in the case of summer rice, the State has attained a normal productivity rate of 1,965 kg per hectare,

District-wise Area, Production and Yield of Rice in Assam during 1990-91 to 1999-2000

Area in '000 Ha | Production in '000 Tonnes | Yield in Kg/Hectare

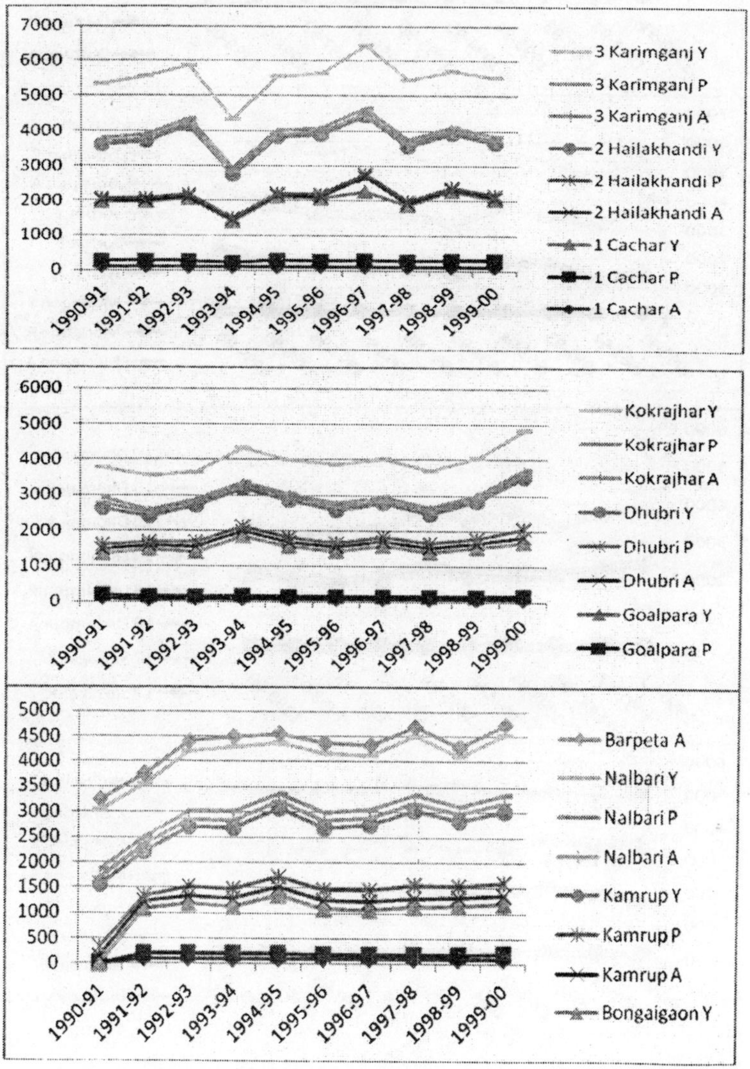

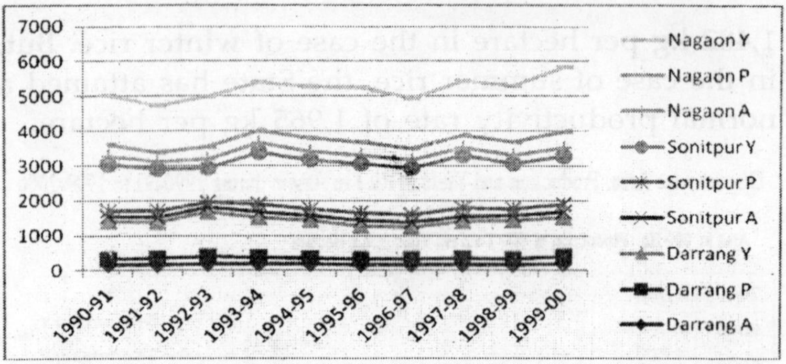
7000
6000
5000
4000
3000
2000
1000
0
1990-91
1991-92
1992-93
1993-94
1994-95
1995-96
1996-97
1997-98
1998-99
1999-00
Nagaon Y
Nagaon P
Nagaon A
Sonitpur Y
Sonitpur P
Sonitpur A
Darrang Y
Darrang P
Darrang A

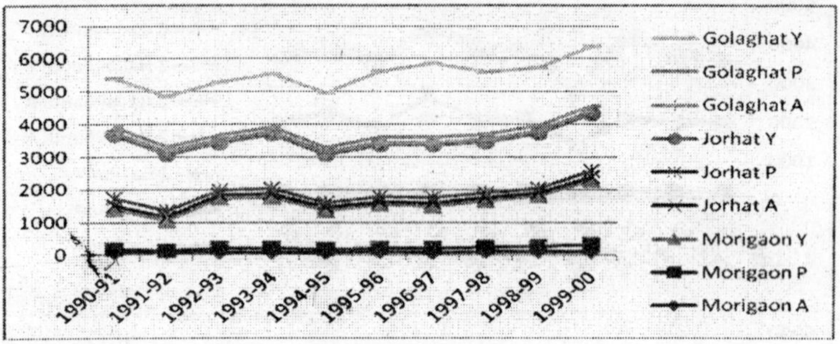
7000
6000
5000
4000
3000
2000
1000
0
1990-91
1991-92
1992-93
1993-94
1994-95
1995-96
1996-97
1997-98
1998-99
1999-00
Golaghat Y
Golaghat P
Golaghat A
Jorhat Y
Jorhat P
Jorhat A
Morigaon Y
Morigaon P
Morigaon A

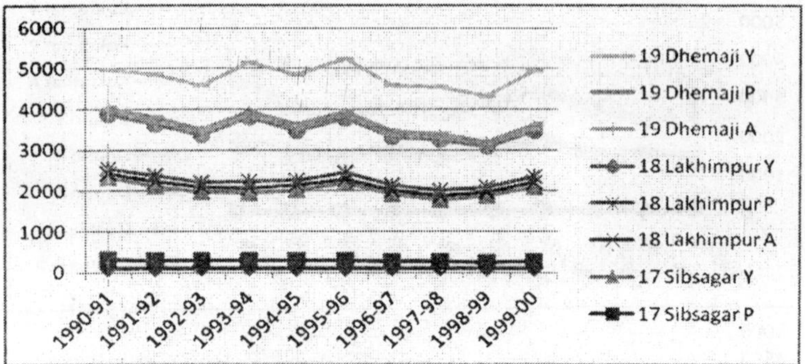
6000
5000
4000
3000
2000
1000
0
1990-91
1991-92
1992-93
1993-94
1994-95
1995-96
1996-97
1997-98
1998-99
1999-00
19 Dhemaji Y
19 Dhemaji P
19 Dhemaji A
18 Lakhimpur Y
18 Lakhimpur P
18 Lakhimpur A
17 Sibsagar Y
17 Sibsagar P

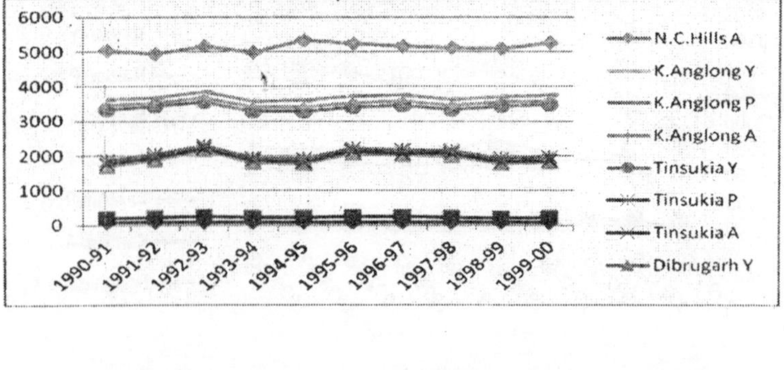
6000
5000
4000
3000
2000
1000
0
1990-91
1991-92
1992-93
1993-94
1994-95
1995-96
1996-97
1997-98
1998-99
1999-00
N.C.Hills A
K.Anglong Y
K.Anglong P
K.Anglong A
Tinsukia Y
Tinsukia P
Tinsukia A
Dibrugarh Y

In India, rice varieties grown in different regions vary with the climatic and soil conditions prevalent there. Often, these varieties are also associated with traditional uses by virtue of being grown in a particular locality for centuries. There are about 200,000 varieties of rice in India, of which 4000 are cultivated. The north-eastern states account for 7.8% of the rice growing area of the country. Assam alone accounts for around 73% of the land under rice cultivation in the North-East. Some varieties of rice traditionally grown in Assam are referred to as komal sawl, or 'soft rice'. These rice varieties need no cooking and soaking them in water will render them fit to be eaten.

In a study conducted by N. Deka in 1999-2000 on the growth and instability of different types of rice, it was found that the growth in the area under summer rice was found to be highest in the state of Assam. Summer rice occupied only marginal area during early and late sixties. At that time, only that low land with enough soil moisture in the rabi season summer rice was grown. Such land can be termed as al Boro area. However during late 70's and 80's this crop became very popular among farmers and it's area increased substantially after creation of irrigation infrastructure in the state. However, for the Hills Zone summer rice did not show significant growth in area, as summer rice was not a very important crop in the hill area. Only in the plain area of Hills zone having adequate soil moisture and low lying areas having irrigation facilities, summer rice is grown. However winter rice was found to be more stable among all the crops with a higher growth in area in Hill Zone. In pooled analysis, production of winter rice revealed a higher growth in upper Brahmaputra valley zone. However winter rice revealed significant growth in production in hill zone and in the state of Assam.

Increase in rice cropped area more particularly Sali rice area appeared to be promising both in Upper Brahmaputra Valley and Hills Zone and in the state of Assam as well. Therefore , steps must be taken to increase the area under Sali rice. Yield of rice could be increased through proper combination of yield increasing crucial input such as HYV seed, irrigation water and fertilizer nutrient. Consumption of fertilizer and quantum of irrigation used are rather low in the study area. Though area under HYV rice in Assam appeared to be satisfactory, yield of rice is comparatively lower than neighboring states. A proper dose of fertilizer and irrigation water in the HYV area could only result in a desired level of yield of rice. Therefore, the personnel of Department of Agriculture and policy makers should create adequate infrastructure for input supply namely irrigation water show that it would facilitate an environment for increased consumption of fertilizer, pesticide and quality seed.

Training should be imparted not only to the farmers but also to the rural youth for increasing the efficiency in allocating and using the available resources, which would enhance the yield of rice. Enhance agricultural production leads to development of value added industries. Though it is not under the purview of study, it might be suggested that, as agriculture is a paying business these days and white colour jobs are scarce day by day, a take off in agriculture would not only help to increase the Net Domestic Product but also boost up the overall economy of the state.

REFERENCES

Aigner, D; Lovell, C. A. K.; and Schmidt, P. 1977. *Formulation and estimation of stochastic frontier production function model.* Journal of Econometrics 6: 21-37.

Ali, M. 1986. *The determinants of inefficiency in Basmati rice production in Pakistan Punjab: Frontier Profit Function Approach.* Ph.D. Dissertation. University of the Philippines.

Ali, M. and Chaudhry, M.A. 1990. *Inter-regional farm efficiency in Pakistan's Punjab: a frontier production function study.* Journal of Agricultural Economics 41(1): 62-74.

Ali, M. and Flinn, J.C. 1989. *Profit efficiency among basmati rice producers in Pakistan's Punjab.* American Journal of Agricultural Economics 71: 303-310

Anderson, R. J.; Dillon, J. L; Hazell, P. B. R.; Cowie, A. J. and wan, G. H. 1988. *Changing variability in cereal production in Australia.* Review of Marketing and Agricultural Economics. 56(3): 270-286

Ballabh, V. and Pandey, S. 1999. *Transitions in rice production system in Eastern India: Evidence from two villages in Uttar Pradesh.* Economic and Political Weekly 34(13): 687-692

Banik, A 1994. *Technical efficiency of irrigated farms in a village of Bangladesh.* Indiiian Journal of Agricultural Economics 49: 70-78

Chand, R. and Tewari, S.C. 1991. *Growth and instability of Indian exports and imports of agricultural commodities.* Indian Journal of Agricultural economics 46(2): 159-165

Coelli, T. and Battese, G. 1996. *Identification of factors which influence the technical inefficiency of Indian farmers*. Australian Journal Agricultural Economics40(2) 103-128.

Das, J. 1995. *Studies on viability and sustainability of specific enterprise based farming system*. Unpublished M. Sc. Thesis, Assam Agricultural University , Jorhat , Assam.

Dawson, P. J. and Lingard, J. 1989. *Measuring farms efficiency over time on Philippine rice farms*. Journal of Agricultural Economics 40(2): 169-177.

Farrell, M. J. 1957. *The measurement of productive efficiency. Journal of Royal Statistical Society*. A 120 part 3: 253-281.

Gajja, B. L.; Sharma, V. P. and Joshi, P. K. 1994. *Productivity variation and land irrigability class in Kakrapar canal command area in Gujarat state*. Indian Journal of Agricultural Economics 49(4): 609-616.

Hazell, P.B.R. 1982. *Instability in Indian foodgrain production*. Research report 30, International Food Policy Research Institute, Washington, USA. pp. 11-60.

Herdt, R. W. and Mandac, A. M 1981. *Modern technology and economic efficiency of Philippine rice farmer*. Economic Development and Cultural Change 29: 375-399.

Hopper, W. D. 1965. *Allocative efficiency in a traditional Indian agriculture*. Journal of Agricultlral Economics 47(3): 611-624.

Huang, C. J.; Tang, A. M. and Bagi, F. S. 1986. *Two views of efficiency of Indian agriculture*. Canadian Journal of Agricultural Economics 34: 209-226.

Jha, B. K. 1994. *Growth and Instability in agriculture associated with new agricultural technology-district level evidence*. Agricultural Situation in India 48: 517-529

Kalirajan, K. P. and Shand, R. T. 1994. *Modelling and measuring economic efficiency under risk*. Indian Journal of Agricultural Economics. 49(4): 579-590.

Kumar, P. and Rosegrant, M. W. 1995. *Trends in rice supply and demand in India. In 'Fragile lives in fragile ecosystem'*. Proceedings of International Rice Research Conference, Feb. 13-17, IRRI, Laguna, Philippines.

Muller, J. 1974. *On sources of measured technical efficiency: The impact of information*. American journal of Agricultural Economics 56: 730-738.

Ravindranath, N.H. et al., *Renewable Energy and Environment*: A Policy Analysis

Reddy, P. P. 1997. *An analysis of inter-regional and temporal variation of costs, productivity and sources of growth of Paddy in Andhra Pradesh*. Indian Journal of Agricultural Economics 52(3): 406-417 for India, Tata McGraw Hill, India, 2000, pp. 41–43.

Shaptadvipa, B. et al., *Asian J. Biochem.*, 2009, 4, 45–54.

Singh, A. J. and Byerlee, D. 1990. *Relative variability in wheat yields across countries and over time*. Journal of Agricultural Economics. 41(1): 21-32.

Smith, K. R. et al., Atmos. Environ., 1983,17, 2343–2362.

Sucharita, G.; Narender, I.; Shuhasini, K and Parthasarathy, P. B. 1995. *Resource use and productivity of turmeric crop in Nizamabad district of Andhra Pradesh*. Agricultural Situation in India 50: 727-730.

Torkamani, J. and Hardaker, J. B. 1996. *A study of economic efficiency of Iranian farmers in Ramjerd district : An application of stochastic programming*. Agricultural Economics 14: 73-83.